Ordinary People

Jorge Consuegra

EXT. BEAUTIFUL COUNTRYSIDE, SMALL TOWN - DAY
Small beautiful country town in the fall, on the shore of a great lake. Close in on school. [Music: Canon in D by Pachelbel, and angel voices singing then:]

CHOIR
(OS: young male voices)
In the silence of our souls, O Lord, we contemplate Thy peace

INT. SCHOOL HALL, CHOIR - DAY
Students' choir rehearsing Canon in D by Pachelbel (not originally written with lyrics). Among many, Conrad is singing. He is just behind Jeannine Pratt. They don't know each other yet.

CHOIR
(girls and boys together)
Free from all the world's desires
Free of fear and all anxiety
Ooooh. Ooooh
Ooooh. Ooooh
Alleluia
Alleluia
Sing Alleluia!
[Close in on Conrad]

INT. CONRAD'S BEDROOM - NIGHT
Conrad suddenly wakes up from nightmare

INT. THEATER PLAY - ON STAGE - NIGHT
A man of fifty is holding his wife's hand over the breakfast table.

MAN
Do you know we've made love one hundred and thirteen times?
We hear laughter (numerous).
MAN (cont'd)
I figured it out on my Bowmar calculator.
Laughter again. The man and the woman are two actors on stage of the local theater. A very conventional play. The set represents an average American kitchen. A man and a woman are having coffee. Man is holding woman's hand.
We gradually discover the audience of the theater.
MAN (cont'd)
To know someone that well is a wonderful thing.
Pause
MAN (cont'd)
Two lumps?
[close in on two couples in the audience] Beth and Calvin and their friends. The women are amused, the men trying to keep awake.

WOMAN
No, one.

MAN
So I don't know everything about you. I don't know your favorite movie stars. I can't remember the name of your favorite perfume. I have racked my brain and I can't remember.

WOMAN
That's funny. It's "My Sin."
Audience laughs, Alvin wakes up and behaves. Gives a conventional smile to his wife Beth.

MAN
But I do know, in the last twenty four years, that I have never been out of love with you.

EXT. THEATER - NIGHT
The four of them come out of the theater. The women walk together in front, men behind.

CALVIN
Well, did we like it?

FRIEND'S WIFE
I loved it.

BETH
Bev Walsh was wonderful.

FRIEND'S WIFE
I liked them all.

CALVIN
It was funny.

FRIEND
It was a comedy. Wasn't it?
Essentially?

FRIEND'S WIFE
Well let's face it: Clyde Banner's getting fat.

BETH
Yes.

FRIEND'S WIFE
He should never turn profile.

CALVIN
Most of us shouldn't turn profile.

INT. CAR. COUNTRY ROAD - NIGHT
Calvin seems stunned.

BETH
What was it you were you thinking about?

CALVIN
When?
Calvin gives his wife a conventional smile. She coddles up against him, but it is cold.

INT. JARRETT'S HOME. - NIGHT
Car enters garage.
[car door Alarm On] / [car door Alarm Off] as car doors open and close.
Beth goes upstairs and directly into her bedroom. Calvin notices this, then notices the light under his son's bedroom door. He knocks.

INT. CONRAD'S BEDROOM - NIGHT
Conrad is lying on his stomach, on his bed, thinking. He composes himself, grabs his book as if he had been reading.

CONRAD
Yeah?
Calvin opens the door, but does not enter the room, respecting his son's privacy:

CALVIN
You okay?

CONRAD
Mmm, mm. Yeah.
How was the show?
Calvin shrugs, as if to say "so and so..."

CALVIN
Mmmh. Trouble sleeping?

CONRAD
No.

CALVIN
You're sure?

CONRAD
Mm-hmm.

CALVIN
Burning the midnight oil?

CONRAD
Yeah.

CALVIN
Okay.
Pause
CALVIN (cont'd)
You thought about calling that doctor?

CONRAD
No.

CALVIN
Well, the month's up. I think we should stick to the plan.

CONRAD
The plan was if I needed to call him.

CALVIN
Yeah. Okay. Don't worry about it.
Get some sleep. By the way, I am working on those Michigan State tickets.

CONRAD
Okay.
Calvin closes the door. Conrad reflects, then shuts off light.

INT. PARENTS' BEDROOM - NIGHT
Calvin shuts off bedside lamp. Then kisses Beth. They embrace.

INT. KITCHEN - MORNING
Beth prepares the breakfast table geometrically (CU).

INT. CONRAD'S BEDROOM - MORNING
Conrad's lies on his bed, fully dressed, full awake, thinking.

BETH
(OS, IN THE KITCHEN)
What about the Warrens, did you call them?

CALVIN
(OS, IN THE KITCHEN)
Yeah, they said they'll make it some evening soon.
Look at these people. Everybody I grew up with... is in the paper these days.

INT. KITCHEN - MORNING
Calvin is reading his newspaper. Beth is preparing the breakfast

CALVIN
"Joey Georgella. New football coach for Trinity."

INT. CONRAD'S BEDROOM - MORNING
Conrad's sits up on his bed.

CALVIN
(OS, downstairs)
Did you check with Jane for the
Michigan State tickets?

INT. KITCHEN - MORNING
Calvin is reading his newspaper. Beth is cooking some French toast.

BETH
Yes. She'll talk to John.
Where's Conrad? This'll get cold.

CALVIN
Con!

INT. CONRAD'S BEDROOM - MORNING
Conrad's sitting on his bed.

CALVIN
(OS, downstairs)
(to Beth)
Will you drop those suits at the cleaners for me?

BETH
They won't be back by Saturday.

INT. KITCHEN - MORNING
Beth still preparing breakfast.

CALVIN
That's okay. Connie!
Calvin goes to the stairs and calls upstairs.

CALVIN (cont'd)
Conrad!

INT. CONRAD'S BEDROOM - MORNING
CONRAD
I'll be right there!

INT. KITCHEN - MORNING
Calvin sits back at table. Conrad finally appears at the bottom of the stairs.

CALVIN
Here he is!

CONRAD
Morning.

BETH
Morning.

CONRAD
Morning.

CALVIN
Did you sleep?

CONRAD
Yeah.

CALVIN
Hungry?

CONRAD
(wondering)
Uh...uh... hungry, uh?
Beth slides a French toast onto Conrad's plate.

BETH
It's French toast. It's your favorite.

CALVIN
Yeah.

CONRAD
Uh... I'm not really hungry.

CALVIN

Breakfast, pal, remember? Main meal. Energy!
Beth comes and takes away Calvin's plate right away.

BETH
You're not hungry, you're not hungry!
Beth takes away the food and goes to throw it away.

CALVIN
Wait a minute, Beth, Hang on. He's gonna eat it. Come on.
(to Conrad)
It's French toast.
Beth pushes the toast in the sink's grinder. French toast disappears.

BETH
There's fresh fruit for you when you get home from school later.
Grinding noise of disposal.

CALVIN
What are you doing? What are you doing?

BETH
You can't save French toast.
BETH (cont'd)
Listen, I've got to run. I'm playing at nine. Will you please call Mr. Herman about the shutters?
I can't get anywhere with that man.
Beth exits.

CALVIN
You have to charm Mr. Herman. Did you charm him?
(to Conrad)
You have to eat, Con. We just want you keep on getting stronger.

CONRAD
Dad, I'm not hungry.

CALVIN
Are you okay?

CONRAD
Yeah. I got to go. Lazenby's picking me up.
Calvin is strangely overenthusiastic.

CALVIN
Oh. Is he? Great!

CONRAD
Why is it great?

CALVIN
Well. I don't see the old gang much anymore. I miss them. Bring them around... Phil, Don, and Dick Van
Buren. We'll play some touch football on the lawn.

CONRAD
See you later.
Exit Conrad. Calvin resumes eating, reflects, then :

CALVIN
Con!
But his son is gone.

EXT. JARRETT'S HOME - MORNING
Calvin walks up the alley to the street. [Horn honks]
Lazenby's car stops, with music playing. Lazenby is driving,
Stillman is with him in the front and Dickie van Buren is at the back.

LAZENBY
(to Stillman)
It's called flake.
Conrad just stands there, waiting.

DICKIE VAN BUREN
Come on, Jarrett! We're late, let's go!

LAZENBY
Jarrett. Come on!
Conrad gets in the car.

INT. LAZENBY'S CAR - MORNING
STILLMAN
Uh, we're late 'cause little
Dickie's mom had to pack his lunch.

DICKIE VAN BUREN
Christ, Stillman! You guys were late at my house. I been up all night studying for this poly-sci exam.

STILLMAN
That guy wants a goddamn personal analysis of it all.
How do you make sense of that crap, anyway?

LAZENBY
You read the crap!

DICKIE VAN BUREN
Oh, shit! When was the last time you read something?

STILLMAN
Yeah. Right! We swim our ass everyday, when are we supposed to study, uh?.

LAZENBY
I swim and I study.

STILLMAN
Get a sense of reality, Lazenby.
(to Conrad))
What you reading?

DICKIE VAN BUREN
(to Lazenby and
Stillman)
Meditation!

CONRAD
Hardy.

DICKIE VAN BUREN
You guys tried meditation?

STILLMAN
Meditation?

LAZENBY
It's just like thinking, Stillman.
No, I don't do it too often.

STILLMAN
(to Conrad)
Ain't that junior English? You got all junior classes this year? They didn't pass you on anything?

LAZENBY
Stillman, you know they don't pass you on... breathing in that dump if you don't take the final.

DICKIE VAN BUREN
Hey, man, get something on that radio, really. You know, I gotta study.

Conrad stares at the barrier, then away.
DICKIE VAN BUREN (cont'd)
Get something lighter for your head.
Car stops at railroad crossing.
DICKIE VAN BUREN (cont'd)

(OS)
I hope it's a long train. I've got to get the stuff down. I'm gonna flunk this test.

LAZENBY
We're going to be late.
Train passes, Conrad stares through it and as in a zoetrope sees glimpses of a graveyard.

.../...
Car slows down near school.
LAZENBY (cont'd)
Does my hair look like shit, doesn't it?

DICKIE VAN BUREN
Yeah.

LAZENBY
Yes, it looks like shit. Thanks.

STILLMAN
Hey, hey, hey! Hey, there's Pratt.

DICKIE VAN BUREN
Look at that ass!

STILLMAN
Let me out, I need a jump.

LAZENBY
No dirty stuff out of the window.

DICKIE VAN BUREN
No dirty stuff?
(to Janine, outside)
Pratt! You have nice ...knees!
Conrad looks at Jeannine seriously.

STILLMAN
Hey. Interested in something.
Jarrett?
She looks back.

SCHOOL - MORNING
A crowd of students entering school.

INT. SCHOOL, CLASSROOM - MORNING
Conrad seems to be day-dreaming, looking outside. Female literature teacher questions about the character of Jude in the story of Jude the Obscure, written by Thomas Hardy.

TEACHER
How about we discuss some theory, here? Conrad, what's your theory on
Jude Fawley? Conrad?
Conrad comes back to it
TEACHER (cont'd)
What's your theory on Jude Fawley?

CONRAD
Uh...

TEACHER
Do you think he was powerless in the grip of circumstances... or could he have helped himself?

CONRAD
I don't... Uh...Powerless? I guess he thought he was, yeah.

JOEL
The guy was a real jerk. He was hung up on what was the moral thing to do. It didn't make any sense.

TEACHER
I think that's a little too easy,
Joel. Paul? What do you think?

PAUL
I found the book hard to follow. I couldn't figure it out.

EXT. SCHOOL STADIUM - DAY
Conrad eats on a bleacher, reflecting, looking at some students training.

INT. SCHOOL CORRIDOR. PHONE BOOTH - DAY
[Telephone Rings OS]
Conrad is calling Dr Berger.

DR BERGER
(OS)
Hello?

CONRAD
Hello.

DR BERGER
Hello?

CONRAD
Uh, Dr. Berger?

DR BERGER
(OS on phone)
Yes?

CONRAD
Hi. This is Conrad Jarrett calling.

DR BERGER
Who?

CONRAD
Conrad Jarrett!
Dr. Crawford at Hillsboro
Hospital gave me your number... and...

DR BERGER
Oh, yes! I'm with a patient now.
Can you call back at two fifteen?

CONRAD
I don't think I'll be free.

DR BERGER
Then give me your number. I'll call you tonite. Hello? Hello?

CONRAD
Uh, that's OK, I'll try to call you back. Thanks.
Conrad hangs up.

INT. SWIMMING POOL - DAY
Conrad with goggles, ready to jump. Swimming training session. Conrad and six others dive. They swim in their lanes.

COACH SALAN
Go!
OK, Come on, now! Move it, you guys! Move it! Keep it going!

Keep it going! Keep it going!
Come on! Keep plugging! Plugging!
Use those legs! Use those legs!
Lazenby, get with it! Jarrett, keep your head down!
Work it out there! Work it! Come on, now! Come on! Push off! Get your head down. Jarrett! Come on!
Keep it up! Keep it going! Dig!
Dig! Dig in there! Come on! Get at it! Push on. Jarrett! Push on!

INT. SWIMMING POOL, LOCKER ROOM - DAY
Conrad slams his locker's door

INT. DINING ROOM - NIGHT
BETH
Was he actually a client of yours?

CALVIN
Well. Regionally.

BETH
It's too bad.

CALVIN
I mean.. it's tragic. Really.
Look at him now. He's lost everything.

BETH
Fish too dry?

CALVIN
It's not too dry.

BETH
They have a new mechanic at C&S.

CALVIN
What happened to little Harry?

BETH
I don't know. I think he took a job in Skokie. Anyway, this new mechanic is so ...awkward.
(to Conrad)
Is that shirt ripped?
Leave it on the table in the hallway.

CALVIN

That girl from the hospital, the one you painted with, she was from Skokie, wasn't she?

CONRAD
Uh, uh.

CALVIN
What was her name?

CONRAD
Karen.

CALVIN
Sharon?

CONRAD
Karen!

CALVIN
Karen.

BETH
Conrad, do you want me to sign you up for round robin at the club?

CONRAD
I haven't played in a year.

BETH
Well, don't you think it's time to start?
Silence
BETH (cont'd)
Also, Calvin, we have to go to the
Murrays on saturday, I couldn't get out of it, it's Clark's birthday. I bought him that book on wine.

CALVIN
(aside)
Good god, not the Murrays...

INT. BEDROOM - NIGHT
Conrad is twisting in his bed under a nightmare
EXT. NIGHTMARE. STORM on LAKE - NIGHT
Conrad and Buck are fighting against the storm in their small sailboat

CONRAD
Lift the rope off Bucky!

INT. BEDROOM - NIGHT
Conrad is twisting in his bed under his nightmare
EXT. NIGHTMARE. STORM on LAKE - NIGHT
Conrad and Buck are fighting against the storm in their small sailboat

BUCK
We're going in!

INT. BEDROOM - NIGHT
Conrad is twisting in his bed under his nightmare
EXT. STORM on LAKE - NIGHT (NIGHTMARE)
Buck is overboard swimming, trying to cling at the overturned small sailboat

CONRAD
(OS)
Give me your hand!

INT. BEDROOM - NIGHT
Conrad is twisting in his bed under his nightmare
EXT. STORM on LAKE - NIGHT (NIGHTMARE)
Conrad is clingin at the keel of the overturned sailboat

CONRAD
Bucky!

INT. BEDROOM - NIGHT
Conrad is twisting in his bed under his nightmare and muttering in his sleep.

CONRAD
Fuck! Fuck! Ha...

EXT. DR BERGER'S OFFICE BUILDING. STREET. - DAY
Conrad, sitting on a bench, looks at Dr Berger's office windows on the other side of street, hesitating to go. He finally crosses the street and enters building.

INT. DR BERGER'S OFFICE BUILDING. LIFT - DAY
Conrad, kind of terrified, rehearses his meeting Dr. Berger:

CONRAD
Oh, hi. How are you? /.../ Oh. I'm fine /.../ Couldn't be better, really. Oh, terrific, yeah.

INT. DR. BERGER'S CORRIDOR - DAY
Conrad sees
- Dr Berger

- on a bell. He rings but another door opens behind him. Dr Berger motions him to come in.

DR BERGER
Ha! Hi! Come in. It's OK, they all do that.
INT. Dr. BERGER'S OFFICE - DAY
Dr BERGER (cont'd)
Jarrett?
Conrad nods.
Dr BERGER (cont'd)
Come in. Sit down.
Dr Berger is fixing an amplifier
Dr BERGER (cont'd)
I just have to... wire some... volume.
Music suddenly blares. Dr Berger stops it.
Dr BERGER (cont'd)
Ah... sorry. Sit down! You've had trouble finding the place?

CONRAD
Not yet.
Dr Berger gives him a second look. Telephone Rings. Dr Berger sits at his desk, looks up file.

DR BERGER
Hmm.... Jarrett. How long since you've been out of the hospital?

CONRAD
A month and a half.

DR BERGER
Feeling depressed?

CONRAD
No.

DR BERGER
On stage?

CONRAD
Pardon me?

DR BERGER
People nervous... treating you like you're ...a dangerous character?

CONRAD
Yeah. I guess a little.

DR BERGER
Are you?

CONRAD
I don't know.
Dr Berger sits at table, looks up another file.

DR BERGER
How long were you in the hospital?

CONRAD
Four months.

DR BERGER
What did you do?

CONRAD
I tried to off myself. Isn't it down there?

DR BERGER
It doesn't say what your method was.

CONRAD
Double-edged Super Blue.

DR BERGER
Oh.
Dr Berger closes file
Dr BERGER (cont'd)
So how does it feel being home?
Everybody's glad to see you?

CONRAD
Yeah.

DR BERGER
Friends?

CONRAD
Yeah.

DR BERGER
OK?
CONRAD
Yeah.

DR BERGER
Everything...

CONRAD
Yeah.

DR BERGER
You're back in school?
Everything okay at school?
Teachers?

CONRAD
Yeah.

DR BERGER
No problems?

CONRAD
Uh-uh.

DR BERGER
So why are you here?
Pause

CONRAD
Uh... I'd like to be more in control, I guess.

DR BERGER
Why?

CONRAD
So people can quit worrying about me.

DR BERGER
Who's worried about you?

CONRAD
My father, mostly. This is his idea.

DR BERGER
What about your mother? Isn't she worried about you, too?

CONRAD
I don't know, listen. You... You're a friend of Dr Crawford, so you're probably all right, but I'll be straight with you, I don't like this already.

DR BERGER
Well, as long as you're straight.

CONRAD
What do you know about me? Have you talked to Crawford?

DR BERGER
Yes. He called me on the phone. He told me your name and... he told me to look for you. And, uh... he said you had a brother who died. A... boating accident, wasn't it? Want to tell me about it?
Silence
Dr BERGER (cont'd)
Well I suppose you talked this over with Crawford at the hospital.
Right?

CONRAD
Right.
Conrad nods.

DR BERGER
How did that go?

CONRAD
It didn't change anything.

DR BERGER
Why do you want to change?

CONRAD
I told you, I'd like to be more in control.

DR BERGER
Why?

CONRAD
I told you, so people can quit worrying about me.

DR BERGER
Well. I'll tell you something. I'll be straight with you, okay? I'm not big on control. But it's your money.

CONRAD
So to speak.

DR BERGER

So to speak.
Okay...
Dr Berger picks up his diary.
Dr BERGER (cont'd)
How's Tuesdays... and Fridays?
Same time.

CONRAD
Twice... a week?

DR BERGER
Well. Control's a tough nut.

CONRAD
I've got swim practice every night.

DR BERGER
Well. That's a problem. How do we solve that?

CONRAD
Guess I'll have to skip practice twice a week, and come here.

DR BERGER
Well. It's up to you.

CONRAD
I don't like being here. I got to tell you I don't like being here at all.
Dr Berger nods.

DR BERGER
Mm-mmm.

INT. DINING ROOM - NIGHT
Beth tidies up some napkins, neatly tied up in rolls in a drawer which she closes (CU). She is in the kitchen, Calvin speaks to her from the dining room table. Conrad is sitting there too, looking at his father.

CALVIN (OS)
I saw Mort Swain. His sister died.

BETH
The one from Idaho?

CALVIN
The one with the restaurant.

BETH
Did she die in Idaho?

CALVIN
I guess so. Why?

BETH
You said she was always traveling.
I just... wondered if she died in
Idaho.

CALVIN
I don't know. Maybe she died in
Idaho. Maybe Kansas City.
Conrad laughs. Calvin too. Calvin is first surprised, then pleased by his son's reaction.

CONRAD
I went to see Dr. Berger.
In the kitchen, Beth stops and listens.

CALVIN
Berger?

CONRAD
Yeah.

CALVIN
Did you?

CONRAD
Yeah.

CALVIN
Good! You didn't say anything.
Good!

CONRAD
I went.

CALVIN
When?

CONRAD
Today.
Beth comes closer

22

BETH
I didn't know you made an appointment.

CALVIN
How did it go?

CONRAD
If it's too much money, I don't have to go. It's not necessary...

CALVIN
(enthusiastic)
Don't worry about the money, it's okay.

CONRAD
Well it's 50 $ an hour. Twice a week.

CALVIN
Ah, it's okay. And it is necessary.
What did you talk about?

CONRAD
Not much.

CALVIN
What about your schedule? Will that be all right?

CONRAD
Well, it'll cut into swim practice.

BETH
Where's his office?

CONRAD
Highland Park.

INT. SWIMMING POOL, POOLSIDE - DAY
COACH SALAN
(screaming at a swimmer)
Keep that head straight Genthe! I don't want to tell you again!
Conrad is standing in front of him shivering from cold.
COACH SALAN (cont'd)
(to Conrad)
Now, this is what I see.
I see you yawning, I see you come late. I don't see you having any fun out there. Are you getting enough sleep?

CONRAD
Yeah.

COACH SALAN
Well, are you having fun out there?

CONRAD
Fun?

COACH SALAN
There's no point if you're not having fun. Right?

CONRAD
Yeah. I guess so.

COACH SALAN
You guess so...? Are you on medication, Jarrett? Tranquilizers? Anything?

CONRAD
No. No, sir.

COACH SALAN
Did I ask you if they gave you shock out there?

CONRAD
Yeah.

COACH SALAN
Yeah what?

CONRAD
Yeah. You asked me. Yeah, they did.

COACH SALAN
Don't look at us, Lazenby! Get your ass in the water! Look at the bottom of the pool! You know, I'm no doctor, Jarrett. I would never have let them put electricity in my head.

EXT. SWIMMING POOL CORRIDOR - DAY
Students coming out of the pool. Lazenby and Dickie, followed by Conrad and Stillman

DICKIE VAN BUREN
God that Salan! He's such a picky bastard! He drives me nuts!

STILLMAN
Everybody drives you nuts.

STILLMAN (cont'd)
Don and Fenetch look good, don't you think, Jarrett?

CONRAD
They look very good.

DICKIE VAN BUREN
Hey, Con, is he giving you a hard time?

LAZENBY
He gives everybody a hard time, Dickie.

JEANNINE'S FRIEND
You guys don't want a clarinet, do you?

STILLMAN
Yeah, Van Buren wants a clarinet.

DICKIE VAN BUREN
I don't need a clarinet. Who's selling it?

JEANNINE'S FRIEND
My brother. He needs a motorcycle.

DICKIE VAN BUREN
Uh, uh... I need a new pair of shoes.

STILLMAN
You need a new personality.
Dickie Van Buren and Stillman leave. Conrad and Lazenby stand in front of Jeannine and her friend.

JEANNINE
(points at Jarrett)
You, you stand behind me in the choir.

CONRAD
Oh? I do? You do? Is that you?

JEANNINE
You have a lot of energy.

CONRAD
I do?

JEANNINE
Yeah. I mean, That's good. My name's Jeannine Pratt.

CONRAD
Nice. Hi!

JEANNINE'S FRIEND
You're Conrad Jarrett, remember?

CONRAD
Right. Hum. Yeah. Um. Bye.

JEANNINE
Bye-bye.

LAZENBY
"You've got a lot of energy."

INT. JARRETT'S HOUSE, ENTRANCE - NIGHT
Halloween : Beth opens door with a plate of candied apples ready. Outside, five kids screaming.

CHILDREN (OS)
Trick or treat!

BETH
You're the scariest ghost I've ever seen! And the tiger and the witch...
You all look just wonderful. Take an apple.

CHILDREN
Thank you.

BETH
There you go. Be careful.

CHILDREN
Thank you Mrs Jarrett, bye.

BETH
Good-bye.
Children's laughs. Beth closes the door.
BETH (cont'd)
The Cabbots. Little Julie's first time. God, she's so cute!

EXT. JARRETT'S HOUSE - NIGHT
The children run away, laughing.

CHILDREN
Ha! Ha! Ha! Ha!

BETH (OS)
Know what I've been thinking?

INT. JARRETT'S HOUSE, LIVING ROOM - NIGHT
Calvin is lying back on the couch. Beth is by his side, and talks to him seducingly.

CALVIN
Mmm?

BETH
That Christmas in London would be like something out of Dickens. We've never done that before, right? Christmas in London?

CALVIN
Maybe we shouldn't plan to go away right now.

BETH
Yes, we talked about that. We decided on that.

CALVIN
Yeah. I know we talked about it, but the more I talk about it, the more the timing doesn't seem right.

BETH
(interrupting)
Calvin, we've always gone away at
Christmas time.

CALVIN
I know.

BETH
I think... I think it would be good for him too. Isn't it time we got back to normal?

CALVIN
He's just started with this doctor.

BETH
Alright, so he'll miss three weeks.
Why interrupt it?
BETH (cont'd)
Because I want to get away! I think we all should. It's important.

CALVIN
No. If he doesn't go through with this now, he might change his mind.

BETH
Alright then if he changes his mind, maybe it's not something that was right for him to do.

CALVIN
You talked to him about it? Does he want to go to London?

BETH
I don't think he knows what he wants to do.

EXT. JARRETT'S HOUSE - DAY
Beth arrives in alley with car, takes out shopping, enters house.

INT. JARRETT'S HOUSE, BEDROOM'S LANDING - DAY
Beth goes upstairs with her shopping, knocks on Conrad's door. No answer. She enters in an authoritarian way, then comes out and closes the door. She then goes to the next door on the landing (Buck's bedroom), stops in front of it. She hesitates, then enters.

INT. JARRETT'S HOUSE, BUCK'S BEDROOM - DAY
Beth slowly enters Buck's abandoned bedroom, all silent.
Everything has stayed like it was. Beth looks around, sits on bed. Stares at photos, prizes and objects. It's like a museum.

EXT. JARRETT'S HOUSE - DAY
Conrad arrives on foot.

INT. JARRETT'S HOUSE, BUCK'S BEDROOM - DAY
Beth in Buck's abandoned bedroom, all silent, sitting on bed.
Conrad appears at door, Beth is startled.

BETH
HA!
CONRAD
Oh, I'm sorry.

BETH
Don't do that!

CONRAD
I'm sorry, I...

BETH

Ha. I didn't think you were here

CONRAD
I'm sorry, I just got in. I didn't...
I didn't know you were here.

BETH
I didn't play golf, today. It's too cold.

CONRAD
How's your golf game?

BETH
I didn't play.

CONRAD
Oh... It did get colder today.

BETH
No, I mean, ...for the year it's colder.

CONRAD
Yeah.
Beth leaves Buck's bedroom.

INT. JARRETT'S HOUSE, LANDING - DAY
BETH
Weren't you swimming today?

CONRAD
Uh-huh. Sorry I scared you.

BETH
How'd it go?

CONRAD
Good. I swam well, today.

BETH
Good.

CONRAD
Yeah.
Personaly I think I could swim the 50 if my timing got...
He leans back against a wardrobe. Beth sees it.

BETH
Off.

CONRAD
...my timing got better.
I'm a just a little... a little off with my... my timing.

BETH
Well, you have to work at that.

CONRAD
Yeah. Oh, I got seventy four on a trig quiz.

BETH
Seventy four? Gee, I was awful at trig.

CONRAD
Oh? Did you...? You took Trig?
Beth stares, trying to remember.

BETH
Wait a minute... Did I take trig?
That's... - uh...? I bought you two shirts. They're on your bed.
Beth enters parents' bedroom and closes the door. Conrad just stands there, paralyzed.

INT. CAR - NIGHT
Beth and Calvin are going to the Murray's birthday party,
Calvin is driving.

CALVIN
Who's gonna be there?

BETH
Well. The Murrays of course, and the Gunthers, and the Caines, and... the good old us.

CALVIN
Why don't we just go to the movies instead?

BETH
Don't be negative.

CALVIN
That's not negative. That's unpredictable.
Come on. Let's really go to the movies.

BETH

Okay.

Calvin smiles, thinking she agrees, not understanding she is taking this as a joke.

CALVIN
Really?

BETH
Okay. Yeah. Come on. Let's go.
What's our excuse?

CALVIN
Beth wanted to go to the movies?

BETH
Good. Very good.
She laughs strangely.

EXT. MURRAY'S HOUSE - NIGHT
The car is arriving at the Murrays' house, we see in background

BETH
All right now, smile.
And remember, not too many martinis.

INT. MURRAY'S HOUSE - NIGHT
Gladyce the maid goes open the door. Beth enters all smiles, followed by Calvin.

BETH
Hello Gladyce. Will you put that with the rest of them?
Several guests. Beth sees Mrs Murray coming down the stairs eyes wide open, showing off.
BETH (cont'd)
Oh, look, we're in time for the grand entrance!

MRS MURRAY
Hello! Look who's here! Three blocks away and the last to arrive.
They kiss.
MRS MURRAY (cont'd)
Come on in.
While going to the dining room, they meet their host, Clark
Murray a thin blond man.

BETH
Clark! Happy birthday! You look wonderful for a 75-year-old!
BETH (cont'd)
Is that new?

MRS MURRAY
Yes. It is. Do you like it?

BETH
You did the mousse?
It turned out well?

CALVIN
Hey. Partner. How are you?
Calvin meets his business associate Ray Hanley, and Man #2 (red tie striped cream, wearing glasses), and their wives.

RAY HANLEY
Hey, pal!
Calvin kisses Ray's wife. Beth is with two women : Woman #1 with dark hair (in green), the other, Woman #2, with grey hair (in orange).

BETH
Hi there.

WOMAN #
Hi. Beth.

BETH
Good to see you, and where were you at the lunch last week?
Man #3 is giving Clark Murray some financial advice

MAN #
Call your bank and borrow the money.

MURRAY
I was thinking of going public.

MAN #
I wouldn't do that, I wouldn't do it now...

MURRAY
Why not?

MAN #
...because the market's low.
Beth is talking to Woman #2 (with grey hair, orange dress)

BETH
Your hair looks wonderful. It's shorter, isn't it? I like that.

Man #2 is telling a joke to two women

MAN #
I said: "Would you please put out your cigar?" and he says: "Huh?". I said: "Would you put out your cigar?", he says: "Huh?". I said:
"Would you please put out your cigar?", he says: " I don't have another one!"
The two women laugh.

BETH
Good to see you! You look beautiful. As ever.

MAN #
(full grey hair)
It's a macho factor. When these kids are at school, they just think they've got to walk on the edge of danger.
Beth joins the two women and man #2 :

BETH
What are these hushed tones all about?

WOMAN #
He just told the funniest joke!
Calvin laughs with two male guests. MAN #4 (with grey hair) passes him

MAN #
I'm not talking to you.

CALVIN
Why?
Woman #2 with grey hair (in orange) is sitting on a couch talking to other guests

WOMAN #
Obviously, you know, I have my fingers crossed on this merger.
Man #3 and Clark Murray are still talking financial advice.

MURRAY
When can we have lunch?

MAN #
Great. Fill me in the office, I have no idea of my schedule, but
I'm free almost everyday.
Calvin talks with Man #2 (red tie striped cream, wearing glasses)

MAN #
I ran into Billy white. Bob Mc
Lean's leaving Coles and Johnson.

CALVIN
Where is he going?

MAN #
He doesn't know.

CALVIN
Jesus.
Beth is laughing, adressing MAN #4 (with grey hair)

BETH
No. You didn't. You're so mean.
Isn't he the meanest man you've met?
A guest, Man #5, talks golf with a woman.

MAN #
When a ball is in play, if a player, his partner, their equipment or their caddies accidentally move it...
Birthday cake comes in with candles (CU)

GUESTS
He's a jolly good fellow
For he's a jolly good fellow
Won't regret, can't forget
What we did for love
Beth and other women and gathered around the piano. They are a little drunk are singing a little false.
Annie, a guest with red blouse, is sitting on the steps of the stairs, eating out of her plate. Calvin comes and sits next to her.

CALVIN
Hi. Annie. What's your boy up to these days?

ANNIE
Oh. Who knows? They won't tell.
How's Conrad doing?

CALVIN
He's great. Just great.

ANNIE
I asked Donald, and he says they haven't talked much. I said maybe he's a little self-conscious.
A woman in green going upstairs, drunk, trips over Calvin

CALVIN
Oh!
Calvin laughs. The woman goes upstairs.
CALVIN (cont'd)
No, no. No. No. He's...
Beth, not far, listens.
CALVIN (cont'd)
There's a doctor in Highland
Park... that he sees a couple of times a week. That kinda cuts into his social life.
Beth, still.
CALVIN (cont'd)
He's great. Just great.

ANNIE
Really? Is he still having some problems?

CALVIN
Oh, no, no. Nothing like that. No, no, just somebody to talk to... that's all. Kind of polish off the rough edges, that's all.
Beth joins in, to cut him off.

BETH
How are you. Darling? Is he falling asleep on you, yet?

ANNIE
Nah. He's great.

CALVIN
(Mimicking "Mr.
Wonderful")
Mr. Great. That's me!

INT. CAR - NIGHT
Beth looks uptight and scornful. Calvin notices it.

CALVIN
Hey?

BETH
You drink too much at parties,
Calvin.

CALVIN
I'm not drunk.

BETH

Why did you tell Annie Marshall that Conrad is seeing a psychiatrist?

CALVIN
I dunno. Why not?

BETH
Well for one thing, I don't think people hear that kind of thing very easily.

CALVIN
Come on, for most people, it's a status symbol, right up there with going to Europe.

BETH
Well, I thought your blurting it out like that was in very bad taste...

CALVIN
I did not think it was that...

BETH
Not to mention a violation of privacy!

CALVIN
Whose privacy?
Beth is strangely vehement.

BETH
Our privacy! The family's privacy!
I think it is a very private matter.
Calvin sighs.
INT. Dr. BERGER'S OFFICE
- DAY
Conrad sits in an armchair, very nervous, scratching his leg.

CONRAD
So what do I do... tell you my dreams?

DR BERGER
I don't hold much stock in dreams.

CONRAD
What kind of a psychiatrist are you? They all believe in dreams.

DR BERGER
Really? What's happening?
What's going on?

CONRAD

I just feel... I feel so...

DR BERGER
What?

CONRAD
Jumpy. I don't know.

DR BERGER
Look. Kiddo... I lied. I do believe in dreams. Only sometimes I want to know what's happening when you're awake. Come on, something's bugging you, making you nervous.
You're making me nervous.

CONRAD
Maybe I need a tranquilizer.

DR BERGER
Tranquilizer?

CONRAD
Yeah.
What do you think?

DR BERGER
I think you came in here looking like something out of The Body Snatchers. It's not my impression that you need a tranquilizer.
Conrad notices a cube on the table.

CONRAD
What is this?

DR BERGER
Clock.

CONRAD
Oh, I see. So you get to tell the time, but I can't. Is that it?

DR BERGER
Mmm, mmm.

CONRAD
So you know when the hour's up?

DR BERGER
Right.

CONRAD
Fifty minutes, fifty five minutes?
What is it?
Dr Berger doesn't answer.
CONRAD (cont'd)
Maybe... Maybe I don't want to swim anymore. You know, I mean my timing is for shit. You know, he's got two guys that swim the fifty, they're better than me, and...

DR BERGER
Ha, ha.

CONRAD
They're a bunch of boring ass jocks.

DR BERGER
Ha, ha.

CONRAD
And him... I can't stand him. He's a tight ass son of a bitch!

DR BERGER
Ah, ah?... Have you ever thought about quitting?

CONRAD
Are you telling me to?

DR BERGER
No.

CONRAD
It wouldn't look good.

DR BERGER
Forget about how it looks! How does it feel?

CONRAD
How does it feel? How does it feel?

DR BERGER
Yes!

CONRAD
How does it feel?!

DR BERGER

Yes! How does it feel?

CONRAD
It's the same thing that happened last year... It's the same damn thing I did last year.

DR BERGER
Are you the same person you were last year?

CONRAD
I don't know!

DR BERGER
That's why you need a tranquilizer?

CONRAD
You tell me!

DR BERGER
No. It's up to you!

CONRAD
Fifty bucks an hour, can't you decide if I should have a pill or not? I mean, you're a doctor, I'm supposed to feel better! Right?

DR BERGER
Not necessarily.
Conrad reflects.
Dr BERGER (cont'd)
How is it with your friends? Is it getting any easier?

CONRAD
No. It's still hard.

DR BERGER
Is anyplace easy?

CONRAD
The hospital was.

DR BERGER
It was? Why?

CONRAD
Because nobody hid anything there.

DR BERGER

Was there anyone there you could talk to?

CONRAD
Uh-huh.

DR BERGER
I mean, besides Dr. Crawford?

CONRAD
Uh-huh.

INT. RESTAURANT - DAY
Conrad is sitting, reflecting. A young woman's hand blinds him for a second : Karen has arrived.

CONRAD
Whoa!

KAREN
Hi!

CONRAD
Hey, Karen! Hi! How are you?

KAREN
Good. Real good.

CONRAD
Sit down. Please.

KAREN
Thank you.

CONRAD
Wow.
Long Pause. They laugh.

KAREN
When did you get back?

CONRAD
Uh... The end of August.

KAREN
God...

CONRAD
It's great to see you.

KAREN
Oh, you too. Listen. I am not gonna be able to stay a real long time.
I've got a meeting over at school.
Drama Club meeting. We're doing "A
Thousand Clowns" this year. You know it? Anyway. We're going so crazy trying to get it together.
I am secretary this year too.

CONRAD
Don't let me hang you up.

KAREN
No. Oh, no, you're not hanging me up! No, I really wanted to see you.
I didn't know quite what to expect, though... I mean, you sounded...uh, you sounded sort of funny on the phone.

CONRAD
(interrupting)
No, no, I wasn't. It was just a gray day, that's all. Kind of...
But everything's great, I'm back in school, I am on the swim team, and...

KAREN
Oh. You're swimming? Terrific,
Conrad! That's... That's really wonderful.

CONRAD
We haven't had any meets yet. I could end up on the bench all year, but...

KAREN
Come on, you'll do great. I'll bet your folks are real proud of you.

CONRAD
Yeah, yeah.

WAITER
What can I get you guys?

CONRAD
You're hungry, at all?

KAREN
Uh... I just want a coke.

CONRAD
Uh... two cokes, please.

KAREN
You think we offended him?

CONRAD
Something I said? Definitely a low self-image day.

KAREN
So. Uh...

CONRAD KAREN
- Are you... - What did...

CONRAD KAREN
I can't believe how beautiful You know what I really wanted you look. to...

CONRAD
You really look beautiful.

KAREN
So do you.

CONRAD
Do you miss it?

KAREN
Miss what?

CONRAD
The hospital.

KAREN
No.
Waiter brings two cokes
KAREN (cont'd)
Thank you.

CONRAD
You don't miss it? At all? Nothing? Nothing about it?

KAREN
No.

CONRAD
You don't miss Leo's corny jokes?
Pause. She looks at him sternly.

KAREN
Are you seeing a doctor?

CONRAD
Yeah. I'm seeing a doctor. Are you?

KAREN
Uh... Uh, well, Dr. Crawford gave me a name, and I went for a while. But uh... I dunno. It just didn't work for me, I guess. He just kept telling me all the things I already knew, and , uh... finally, I decided... the only one who can help me is myself. At least, that's what my dad says.
I don't mean it's not right for you, Conrad. I mean I think that if it's something you want to do, that's what you should be doing.

CONRAD
Well, ya, I don't know how long
I'll keep it up. I sorta got shoved into it.
Pause

KAREN
Your hair grew in.

CONRAD
Oh, yes. That was such a dumb thing to do.

KAREN
I like it.

CONRAD
You do?

KAREN
Yeah!

CONRAD
I don't know, I just... Uh...
I miss it sometimes, the hospital.
Really do.

KAREN
Things have to change. You know?

CONRAD
But that's where we had the laughs.

KAREN
But that was a hospital. This is the real world.

CONRAD
Yeah, yeah, I... you're sure right.
Pause

KAREN
I really have to go. I'm sorry. I have a meeting over at the school.
Drama Club meeting. We're doing "A
Thousand Clowns".

CONRAD
I know, you told me.

KAREN
Did I?

CONRAD
Yeah.

KAREN
I better hurry. Don't wanna be late.

CONRAD
Thanks for seeing me.
He clears his throat.

KAREN
Conrad? Let's have a great
Christmas! Okay? Let's have... a great year. Let's have the best year of our whole lives, OK? We can, you know. This could be the best year ever.

CONRAD
Yeah... Yeah.

KAREN
Yeah!
She gets up
KAREN (cont'd)
Mmm... Will you call me?

CONRAD

Yeah...

KAREN
You mean it?

CONRAD
Yep!

KAREN
You. Uh... You look good. Conrad.

CONRAD
Yeah.

KAREN
Bye.

CONRAD
Bye-bye.
She leaves. Then stops a few steps away, and shouts :

KAREN
Hey!
A customer is startled.
KAREN (cont'd)
Would you cheer up?
Conrad sits there with a strange feeling of embarrassment, reflecting.

EXT. JARRETT'S HOUSE. GARDEN - DAY
From inside, Beth stares outside in the garden where Conrad is lying on a chaise lounge. She comes out.

BETH
It's cold out here. You should put that on, or do you want a sweater?

CONRAD
Do I need one?
Beth is taken off guard by Conrad's reaction, doesn't know what to do.

BETH
What are you doing?

CONRAD
Nothing. Thinking.

BETH

About what?

CONRAD
Not about anything.

BETH
Your hair is starting to grow out.
It's looking... looking better.
Pause

CONRAD
I was thinking about the pigeon...
You know the one that used to hang around the garage. How it used to get on top of your car, and he take off when you pulled out of the driveway.

BETH
Oh. Yeah, I remember. I remember how scared I used to get... That whosssshhhhh! Flap, flap, flap, flap!... Every time I started the car.

CONRAD
Yeah. That was the closest we ever came to having a pet. You remember
Buck asked you, he tried to talk you into... getting a dog. Do you remember that?
He said. "How about it, if it's the size of a little football?"

BETH
You know. Uh... That animal next door, that Pepper or Pippin, whatever its name is...

CONRAD
Pippin. Pippin. Pippin!

BETH
He's not a very friendly dog... I...
I don't care what Mr. McGreary says.

CONRAD BETH
- What he really wanted was a - Everytime time that dog retriever. It was down the comes into this backyard, I street for sale. That's what try to get him out... he wanted. A retriever.

CONRAD
(he barks)
Arf! Arf! Arf!
Beth stops in her tracks, startled, but doesn't show it.

BETH
Put that on if you're gonna stay out here, okay?

Conrad stays alone a while and stares. Then goes inside.

INT. JARRETT'S HOUSE. DINING ROOM - DAY
Conrad enters hesitantly, back from garden. Beth is busy dressing up the table.

CONRAD
Can I help?

BETH
Help what? Oh, you mean with this?
No.

CONRAD
I will.

BETH
(casually)
No, I tell you what you can do though. You can go upstairs to that room of yours and clean out the closet.

CONRAD
Mom...

BETH
Okay? Because it really is a mess.
They stand there, facing each other, uptight. The telephone rings. Beth goes over to it, picks it up, seems suddenly delighted.
BETH (cont'd)
Hello. /.../
Oh, hi! /.../
Yeah, , no, I didn't get there. I was swamped with work. How did it go? /.../
No, no, I'm not doing anything, just getting ready for dinner.
Uh-huh.
Beth laughs to a gossip. Conrad is devastated.
BETH (cont'd)
Did she really?
Beth laughs again.
[echo effect to get into Flashback]

EXT. JARRETT'S HOUSE, GARDEN - DAY
Beth is laughing at Buck story. She is lying leisurely on a mattress on the lawn. Buck is standing, telling his story.

BUCK
Oh anyway, Mary Ann Ramon started to just scream, just cry, right?

It was crazy. We got so drunk that we couldn't talk to each other. It was the last day...
the last day of school.
A younger Conrad, sitting aside, is listening too, amused.
BUCK (cont'd)
We walked out of the building in the middle of the class!
Conrad laughs. Beth laughs.

BETH
Oh, Bucky!
Beth laughs.

INT. JARRETT'S HOUSE, DINING ROOM - DAY
Beth laughs. Conrad stares at Beth laughing on the phone. The gossip gets too funny.

BETH
No. Stop!
Beth laughs.
INT. Dr. BERGER'S OFFICE
- EVENING

DR BERGER
What do you expect from her?

CONRAD
We just don't connect.

DR BERGER
Why not?

CONRAD
I don't know. We just don't.
Silence

DR BERGER
What are you thinking?

CONRAD
That I jack off a lot.

DR BERGER
So what else is new? Does it help?

CONRAD
For a minute.
Silence

DR BERGER
What now?

CONRAD
John Boy.

DR BERGER
Who?

CONRAD
You know, in "The Waltons". John Boy?

DR BERGER
Yeah. What about him?

CONRAD
My father came into my room and he didn't know what to say.
This is right after Buck died.
And he came over and sat on the bed next to me, put his arm around my shoulder. We just sat there.
I remember I was watching his shoe.
And thinking...
Cos his shoe was turned over on its side.
I was thinking: "He's so uptight, it's gonna crack off."
Dr Berger listens carefully.
CONRAD (cont'd)
And I knew I should have felt something.
But I didn't know what to feel.
I kept thinking what they say on
TV, you know, stuff like:

(MORE)
CONRAD (cont'd)
"Oh, no, noo! Ooh, My god!"
But I didn't say that... because
I didn't feel sad... so much as...
Conrad sighs.

DR BERGER
So much as what?

CONRAD
I dunno. I kept thinking that John
Boy would've said something...about the way he felt, you know.
Something.

DR BERGER
What would John Boy have said?

CONRAD
I don't know.

DR BERGER
Come on.
Conrad seems lost. Dr Berger is on to something.
Dr BERGER (cont'd)
Come on.

CONRAD
Come on what?

DR BERGER
Don't hold back.
Silence

EXT. CITY BUSINESS CENTER - DAY
Calvin walks with his business partner Ray Hanley (seen at the party).

RAY HANLEY
Well. At least she's an improvement. She doesn't crack gum in your face. That's what you get when your partner does the hiring and firing.

CALVIN
Oh, I'm sorry. That's my fault.
I just can never seem to tell anybody that they're not making it.

RAY HANLEY
Hold, hold it. Wait a minute.
That's not the problem.
Where are you?

CALVIN
What?

RAY HANLEY
I've been losing you these days.

CALVIN
Oh, I'm sorry.

RAY HANLEY

That's okay. That's okay. You off the track?

CALVIN
Huh?
They laugh.

RAY HANLEY
Come on. I've known you for twenty years. You think I can't tell when something's wrong? How's Connie?

CALVIN
Connie's all right. He is. He's okay.

RAY HANLEY
Look, I am sorry, it's none of my business, but I think you worry too much. You've been on the rack about him long enough. You're making it a habit. You've gotta let him go sometime.

CALVIN
I'm not on the rack about him.

RAY HANLEY
The thing about it is, in a year he'll be gone. Off to Michigan or
Harvard or wherever in the hell he gets it in his head he wants to go.
Maybe he'll decide to take a tour of Europe for a year and not even go to school at all. Who knows?

CALVIN
I can't argue with "Who knows."

RAY HANLEY
I'm just try giving you the benefit of my experience.

CALVIN
Thanks.

RAY HANLEY
With Valerie, it's more than her living away from home... She's gone. Got her own friends, her own life. She breezes in ...for a couple of days on vacations, but... I don't know, maybe girls are different.
Or maybe she was too aware of what was happening between Nance and me.
But they leave... And all that worrying doesn't amount to a hill of crap. It's just wasted energy.
Calvin is troubled.

INT. COMMUTER TRAIN - NIGHT

Going home on the commuter, Calvin is thoughtful. He remembers his sons when they were kids.

INT. JARRETT'S DINING ROOM - DAY
YOUNG CONRAD
Give me back my sweater! Come on, it's my sweater!

YOUNG BUCK
Possession is nine tenths...

CALVIN
Hang on!

YOUNG BUCK
Dad, what's possession?

YOUNG CONRAD
Give it to me!

YOUNG BUCK
I can't, it's already on me.

CALVIN
Wait, hang on! Whose sweater is it?

YOUNG CONRAD
It's my sweater!

YOUNG BUCK
OK! Alright! I'll give it back to you... as long as you give me back my hockey stick and my skis.

YOUNG CONRAD
All right.
Calvin laughs

CALVIN
That's fair!
In the commuter train Calvin also remembers...

INT. JARRETT'S HOME. LANDING - NIGHT
Calvin knocks violently on Conrad's bedroom door

CALVIN
Conrad! Conrad!

BETH
What is it?

EXT. JARRETT'S HOME. STREET - NIGHT
Conrad is taken away on a stretcher into an ambulance.

AMBULANCE MAN
Watch your back. Cuts are vertical.
He really meant business.
WS on Beth, hand on mouth, astonished. Beth and Conrad have overheard.
AMBULANCE MAN (cont'd)
Let's go.

INT. COMMUTER TRAIN - NIGHT
CONDUCTOR
Lake Forest is next. Lake Forest.
Calvin realizes he has to get off.

INT. SWIMMING POOL - NIGHT
Another training session at the swimming pool. Conrad is heavily swimming in his lane, although he looks tired and bored, not really fit for training. He stops, exhausted at the end of a row, looks at his friends happily discussing by the side of the pool, then at coach Salan in his office glass booth overlooking the swimming pool. Conrad reflects.

INT. SWIMMING POOL. COACH SALAN'S OFFICE BOOTH - NIGHT
Coach Salan is sermonning Conrad in his office glass booth overlooking the swimming pool.

COACH SALAN
What it is you want?
I don't know what else to do for you.

CONRAD
I'm not asking you for anything.

COACH SALAN
You gotta be kidding me. I don't get it. I excuse you from practice twice a week so you can see some shrink. I work with you every damn night at your convenience. What the hell more am I supposed to do for you?

CONRAD
Nothing.

COACH SALAN
Bright kid like you, everything going for you. See, I don't get it.
Why do you wanna keep messing up your life?

CONRAD
I don't think that ...that quitting swimming will mess up my life. I... I really don't.

COACH SALAN
Okay. Okay. Now, this is it.

CONRAD
Yeah.

COACH SALAN
You're a big kid now.

CONRAD
Uh, uh.

COACH SALAN
Actions have consequences.

CONRAD
Okay!

COACH SALAN
I'm not taking you back again.
You'll remember that?

CONRAD
I won't ask you to ...sir.
Conrad stands up and leaves. Coach Salan is disappointed.

INT. LOCKER ROOM - NIGHT
[Laughter]
Conrad tidies his closet. Lazenby comes to him.

LAZENBY
What happened? You all right?

CONRAD
Yeah.

LAZENBY
Salan says you quit the swim team.

CONRAD
Yeah.

LAZENBY
Why?

CONRAD
I don't know. I felt like it was a bore.

LAZENBY
That's not a real reason!

CONRAD
Well, that's the way it is.

LAZENBY
So what's going on?

CONRAD
Nothing.

LAZENBY
What happened?

CONRAD
Nothing.

LAZENBY
Connie, come on, talk to me.

CONRAD
Nothing. Swimming's a bore. That's all.

LAZENBY
Well listen, I talked to Salan...

CONRAD
Well, quit talking to people! Okay?

LAZENBY
Holy shit! Yeah. Sure. Fuck you.
Jarrett.
Lazenby walks away to the others, waiting. They leave.

STILLMAN
Ooh! Ohh!

LAZENBY

Shut up. Leave it alone.

STILLMAN
I told you. The guy's a flake.
They laugh. Conrad, angry with himself, slams his locker's door.

INT. DR BERGER'S OFFICE - EVENING
Conrad reclining on couch. Dr Berger washes his hands in background room, then comes in.

DR BERGER
So, what did your dad say about it?

CONRAD
I haven't told him yet.

DR BERGER
How come?

CONRAD
I don't know. The timing isn't right, you know. He sweats everything so much, he'll just get worried about it.

DR BERGER
Can you tell your mother?

CONRAD
My mother? My mother and I don't connect. Don't you listen? I told you that.

(MORE)
CONRAD (cont'd)
What do people have in common with mothers anyway? It's all surface junk. You know: "Clean your room, brush your teeth, get good grades, nah, nah, nah, veh..."
Hey, look, I'm just wasting money today. I am not gonna feel anything. I'm sorry.

DR BERGER
No. Sorry's out. Come on, something's on your mind.

CONRAD
What time is it?

DR BERGER
No, no, never mind the time.
There's time. Look. Remember the contract? Control? Maybe there's some connection between control and uh... -
what do we call it? - lack of feeling? Mmm?

CONRAD
I said I feel things.

DR BERGER
When?

CONRAD
Ah, God... Come on.

DR BERGER
When?

CONRAD
Sometimes. I don't know.

DR BERGER
Come on, come on, Jarrett, I thought you didn't like to fool around.

CONRAD
I don't? I'm not.

DR BERGER
Like to play games, do you?

CONRAD
I don't!

DR BERGER
So?

CONRAD
What do you want?

DR BERGER
I'll tell you what I want. I want you to leave "I don't know" out there on the table with the magazines. Okay?

CONRAD
Yeah, and if I don't have an answer you want me to make one up?

DR BERGER
Yeah. That would be nice. Make one up. Right now. About how there's no feelings in there.

CONRAD

I said I have feelings.

DR BERGER
Oh! Now you have, now you don't!
Get it together, Jarrett.

CONRAD
Why you hassle me? Why are you trying to make me mad?

DR BERGER
Are you mad?

CONRAD
No!

DR BERGER
Oh, cut the shit! You're mad!
You're mad as hell! You don't like being pushed.
So why don't you do something about it!

CONRAD
What?

DR BERGER
Tell me to fuck off! I don't know.

CONRAD
Well, fuck off! No. No, I can't, I can't do this.

DR BERGER
Why not?

CONRAD
I can't...

DR BERGER
Why not?

CONRAD
I can't do this. It takes too much energy to get mad!

DR BERGER
Do you know how much energy it takes to hold it back?

CONRAD
When I let myself feel low, I feel as lousy.

DR BERGER
Oh! I beg your pardon! I never promised you a rose garden...

CONRAD
Fuck you. Berger!

DR BERGER
What?

CONRAD
Fuck you.

DR BERGER
Yeah?

CONRAD
Fuck you!

DR BERGER
That's it!

CONRAD
Jesus, you're really weird! What about you? What do you feel, huh? Do you jack off or jerk off? Whatever you call it?

DR BERGER
What do you think?

CONRAD
(shouts at him)
What do I think? I think you married your fat lady... and you goona over fuck the daylights out of her!

DR BERGER
Sounds good to me.

CONRAD
Ah! Ha! Ha...
Conrad falls on the couch, out of breath.

DR BERGER
A little advice about feeling, kiddo... Don't expect it always to tickle.

INT. GRANDPARENTS' LIVING ROOM - DAY

Beth, Grandfather (Beth's father), Conrad and Calvin pose in front of Grandmother (Beth's mother) aiming her camera to take a photo. Grandfather is very excited and noisy.

GRANDFATHER GRANDMOTHER
Ha! Ha! Mother do you know Be quiet. I have to how to aim that thing? concentrate. Be quiet.

GRANDFATHER GRANDMOTHER
Is it in focus? Smile. Smile. Okay. Good.
Okay, now I want to take the three young ones. Dad, will you get out of there. Will you get out of there?

GRANDFATHER
Oh, all right, all right.

GRANDMOTHER
And be quiet. Be quiet. Be quiet.
Conrad. Where are you?

GRANDFATHER
Connie!

GRANDMOTHER
Connie.

GRANDFATHER
Over in the middle between your mother and father.

CALVIN
That's good.

GRANDMOTHER
That's great. All right, smile everybody.

GRANDFATHER GRANDMOTHER
You're taller than your Quiet! Will you be quiet? mother is! Really! All right, smile!

GRANDFATHER GRANDMOTHER
This is beautiful. Hold it Shut up! Wonderful. OK, now I level, would you? want to take Cal and Beth.

OK?
GRANDFATHER GRANDMOTHER
Great! Sure. Oh, come on. You Oh, hoooold it! can do better than that.

GRANDFATHER
Ohhh!

CALVIN
Connie. I want one of Connie and his mother.

BETH
No, I tell you what. Let's get the three men in there, and I'll take a picture of you.

CALVIN
Connie, move in a little closer to your mother. Okay... prize winner...

GRANDFATHER
Yeah. That's great.

CALVIN
Portrait...

GRANDFATHER
It's great.

BETH
Do it.

CALVIN
Page one, Lake Forrester...

GRANDFATHER GRANDMOTHER
Ain't it mother? Yes. It's marvellous. I love it.
Calvin clicks but it doesn't work, the camera wasn't cocked.
CALVIN (cont'd)
Shoot, I didn't cock it.

BETH
Calvin...

CALVIN
Hold it. Connie, smile!

BETH
Calvin!

CALVIN
Just a second, smile!

BETH

Calvin, give me the camera.

CALVIN
No, I didn't get it yet , Beth.

BETH
Come on, give me the camera.

CONRAD
Dad, give her the camera.

CALVIN
I want a really good picture of the two of you, OK?

BETH
No but I really want a shot of the three of you men. Give me the camera, Calvin. Please...

CALVIN
Not until I get a picture of the two of you.

BETH
Cal?

CONRAD
(shouts)

GIVE-HER-THE-GODDAMN-CAMERA!
Calvin is startled. Conrad sits in an armchair. Calvin hands the camera to Beth. They exchange places.

BETH
Smile.
Beth takes a photo of Calvin.
BETH (cont'd)
Who's hungry? I'll make the sandwiches.
Beth leaves for the kitchen, leaving the camera to her mother.

INT. GRANDPARENTS' KITCHEN - DAY
[plate crashes]. We follow the grandmother going to the kitchen to see what's happening. With her, we discover Beth kneeling, picking up a broken plate on the ground.

GRANDMOTHER
Beth?!

BETH

I think it can be saved.
Beth gets up, goes to the table and starts preparing the sandwiches.
BETH (cont'd)
That was dumb. It was just so dumb.
I don't think he's happy in school.

GRANDMOTHER
Have you talked to his teachers?

BETH
I don't think people want to be with him. He provokes people.

GRANDMOTHER
Well. / Why don't you do this? /
It's an awkward age.

BETH
Thank you.

GRANDMOTHER
Maybe he needs a change. Are you sure he's eating enough?

BETH
Yes, Mother, of course.

GRANDMOTHER
I think he'll be all right - if you're firm with him, mmm?

BETH
I think maybe he should go away to school. I just don't know how to deal with him any more.

GRANDMOTHER
Who would make that decision?

BETH
I don't know. I suppose this doctor he's seeing.

GRANDMOTHER
What sort of doctor... would make that decision for you?

BETH
A psychiatrist.

GRANDMOTHER
I thought we were all finished with that.

BETH
No...

GRANDMOTHER
What's his name?

BETH
Berger.

GRANDMOTHER
Jewish doctor?

BETH
I dunno, I suppose he's Jewish.
Maybe just German.

GRANDMOTHER
What does Cal say about all this?
Beth shows her mother the two pieces of the plate and puts them together.

BETH
You know, I think this can be saved. It's a nice clean break.

INT. SCHOOL - EVENING
The choir is rehearsing.

CHOIR
Alleluia, Amen. Amen. Alleluia,
Amen. Aaaaaamen.
(final)

CONDUCTOR
Okay. Altos, that last "E" natural could be just a little higher.
Officers, don't forget your meeting tonight. That's it.
Choir breaks. Jeannine looks at Conrad.

INT. SCHOOL CORRIDOR - EVENING
Jeannine in school corridor still singing.

JEANNINE
Mmm mm mmm, Mmm mm mmm, Mmm mmm
Mmm mm mmm.
Jeannine stops to drink some water at the tap of the fountain. Conrad see her when he is already too near, and has almost his coat on. Seeing an opportunity to talk to her, he

steps back, takes off his coat while she is not looking, then passes her, putting on his coat as if he was naturally on his way out.

GIRLS
Hi. Jeannine!
Jeannine notices Conrad passing by.

JEANNINE
You are really a terrific tenor.

CONRAD
Oh...

JEANNINE
In fact. You should be doing the solo in that Russian thing.

CONRAD
Ha, no. I...

JEANNINE
No. I'm serious. You really sing well. I'm getting to know your voice.

CONRAD
Yeah?

JEANNINE
Yeah!

CONRAD
How can you hear me sing if you're singing?

JEANNINE
Well... I don't always sing.
Sometimes I just listen.

CONRAD
Oh?

JEANNINE
For instance, Marcia Blair can't sing a note.

CONRAD
Uh, uh...

JEANNINE
Janet Fox only mouths the words and never sings.

CONRAD
Ha, ha? Ha, a detective?

JEANNINE
Yeah...

EXT. PARK - EVENING
JEANNINE
Do you like Vivaldi?

CONRAD
Uh...

JEANNINE
Telemann?

CONRAD
Telemann? Um...

JEANNINE
What kind of music do you like?

CONRAD
Oh. Uh... Modern jazz. I like. Folk rock. Spoon on a glass.

JEANNINE
Spoon on a ...glass?
Conrad laughs.
JEANNINE (cont'd)
Oh, you mean like ...tablespoon?
Oh, dear! Why do I ask dumb questions? I'm just showing off.
Why is it so hard... the first time you talk to somebody?
Conrad shrugs.

CONRAD
Mmmm. You make it look easy.
Jeannine is touched.

JEANNINE
Really?
Jeannine looks at him, then:
JEANNINE (cont'd)
Oh, that's my bus, I got to go!
She runs and gets into the bus. Conrad follows and see her gets into the bus.
JEANNINE (cont'd)

I'll see you later!
And you're really a terrific tenor!

CONRAD
(singing like a tenor)
Ah. You're just saying that?
Bus goes away.
CONRAD (cont'd)
Alleluia! Alleluia!

EXT. PARK - EVENING
Conrad goes home through park.

CONRAD
Alleluia! Ah ha, ha, ha, ha, ha, ha, ha. Ha, ha, ha, ha, ha, ha, ha, ha, ha, alleluia! Alleluia! Alleluia, Alleluia! Alleluia!
Alleluia! Alleluia! Alleluia!

INT. CONRAD'S BEDROOM - EVENING
Conrad enters his room still singing in a low voice.

CONRAD
Alleluia!
He browses quickly through a pocket book, finds the piece of paper inserted in it, picks up phone and dials the number written on the paper

KAREN'S MOTHER
Hello?

CONRAD
Hello. Is Karen there?

KAREN'S MOTHER
Who's calling, please?

CONRAD
It's a friend of hers from
Hillsboro?

KAREN'S MOTHER
Oh... Well, she's ...not home from school yet.

CONRAD
Oh. Um...Hmm. Just tell her I called. This is Conrad. Calling.
Just tell her I called and I'm feeling great, and I just wanted to talk to her.

KAREN'S MOTHER
Yes. I will.

CONRAD
OK. Thank you.

KAREN'S MOTHER
Good bye.
Conrad walks nervously around to and fro for a while then looks up into directory. He finds Jeannine number, writes it down "Pratt 5556719", then picks up the phone.

CONRAD
All right
Conrad hangs up, and rehearses what he is going to say, but he is yet too shy to call.
CONRAD (cont'd)
Hello. Jeannine. This is Conrad.
Hello. Jeannine, this is Conrad.
Hello. Jeannine. This is Conrad.
Conrad. Conrad? What a dumb name.
Hello. Jeannine. This is Bill.
Uuuuurgh!
Conrad takes courage and dials Jeannine number.

JEANNINE
Hello?

CONRAD
Hello. This is... Hello, this is
Conrad calling. Jarrett?

JEANNINE
Oh...
(realizing, more enthusiastic)
Oh. Hi!

CONRAD
Hi. Listen. I was... I was wondering if maybe you'd like...to go out sometime?

JEANNINE
You mean, with you? Like on a date?

CONRAD
Well, yeah, we wouldn't have to call it a real date. We could fake it sort of, to see how it goes..
Jeannine laughs.

JEANNINE
That was dumb. Forget it. Just forget it. Now start over.

CONRAD
Hi, this is Conrad Jarrett...

JEANNINE
(interrupting))
I'd love to. When?
Conrad laughs.

EXT. STREET JARRETT'S HOME - DAY
[Happy music] Calvin and Conrad happily come back home with a Christmas tree on top of car.

INT. JARRETT'S LIVING ROOM - DAY
Christmas tree standing in living room ready to be decorated.
Bet silently comes in. Calvin finally notices she is here.

CALVIN
I didn't see you there. What do you think?

BETH
(cold)
Fine.

CALVIN
Rawlins used to have such great
Scotch pines. And they all look like skeletons this year.
Conrad comes in with a box of chritsmas tree decorations

CONRAD
Hi. What do you think?

BETH
(cold)
Very nice.
Conrad and Calvin stop at the tone of her voice.

CALVIN
What's wrong?

BETH
(cold)
Why don't you ask him what's wrong?
Maybe you won't have to hear it from Carol Lazenby.

CALVIN
Hear what?

CONRAD
Dad, I quit the swim team.

CALVIN
What?

BETH
Carol thought I knew. Cos why wouldn't I? It happened over a month ago.

CALVIN
Quit? When? Where have you been every night?

CONRAD
Nowhere. Around. The library mostly.

CALVIN
Why didn't you tell us, Connie?

CONRAD
I don't know, I didn't think it mattered.

CALVIN
What do you mean? Why wouldn't it matter? Of course it matters. And...

BETH
(interrupting)
No, that was meant for me, Calvin.

CALVIN
What was meant for you?

BETH
It's really important to try to hurt me. Isn't it?

CONRAD
Don't you have that backwards?

BETH
Oh? And how do I hurt you? By embarrassing you in front of a friend? Poor Beth! She has no idea what her son is up to! He lies and she believes every word of it.

CONRAD
I didn't lie!

BETH
You did! You lied everytime you came into this house at 6:30 !
If it's starting all over again, the lying, the covering up, the disappearing for hours, I will not stand for it! I can't stand it! I really can't!

CONRAD
Well don't then! Go to Europe!

CALVIN
Connie! Now, Connie! Connie!...

CONRAD
Cos the only reason she cares, the only reason she gives a fuck about it...

CALVIN
Connie!...

CONRAD
...is because someone else knew about it first!

CALVIN
Just stop it, Connie! ...

CONRAD
No! You tell her to stop it! You never tell her a godamn thing!
And I know why she never came to the hospital, she's busy going to goddamn Spain and... goddamn
Portugal! Why should she care if
I'm hung up by the balls out there?

BETH
Maybe this is how they sit around and talk at the hospital, but we're not at the hospital now.

CONRAD
You never came to the hospital!

CALVIN
How do you know she never came?
You know she came but she had the flu and couldn't come inside, but she came.

CONRAD
Yeah! She wouldn't have had any flu if Buck was in the hospital!

She would have come if Buck was in the hospital!

BETH
Buck never would've been in the hospital!
Conrad takes his head between his hands and runs upstairs.

CALVIN
That's enough! That is enough!

BETH
I won't do it again. I really won't do it.

CALVIN
What in hell has happened?
Upstairs, Conrad's bedroom door slams.
CALVIN (cont'd)
Somebody better go up there.

BETH
Ah! Oh, god, that's the pattern, isn't it? He walks all over us and then you go up and apologize to him.

CALVIN
I am not going to apologize...

BETH
Yes of course you are! You always do! You've been apologizing to him ever since he got home from the hospital, only you don't see it!

CALVIN
I am not apologizing. I'm trying to goddamn understand him!

BETH
Don't talk to me that way. Don't you talk to me the way he talks to you!

CALVIN
Beth. Let's not fight. Okay? No fighting. Okay? Please. Let's go upstairs.
Calvin goes, but Beth doesn't, and turns away.

INT. CONRAD'S BEDROOM - EVENING
Calvin enters Conrad's bedroom and closes the door. Conrad is lying on his stomach, feeling all crooked. His voice is muffled by his head between his arms.

CALVIN
I want to talk to you.

CONRAD
I need to sleep.

CALVIN
In a minute...

CONRAD
I didn't mean it. I didn't mean any of it. I am sorry. Please don't be mad.

CALVIN
I'm not mad ! I'm just trying to figure out what happened down there.

CONRAD
I don't know what happened! I am sorry about it all. I am sorry about the whole thing. What I said, I didn't mean it. Just please tell her. Tell her I'm sorry, will you?

CALVIN
Why don't you tell her?

CONRAD
Oh, God, no, I can't! Don't you see? I can't talk to her!

CALVIN
Why not?

CONRAD
Ha! Because it doesn't change anything. It doesn't change the way she looks at me.

CALVIN
She was upset, Conrad. Your mother was hurt because you quit the swim team. I don't understand it myself.

CONRAD
I don't mean just now. Don't you see? I don't mean just today.

CALVIN
What then? Explain it to me.

CONRAD
Ha! I can't! Everything is German pudding with you , dad. You don't see things!

CALVIN
What things?
Conrad sighs.
CALVIN (cont'd)
What things? Please, I want you to tell me.

CONRAD
That she hates me! Can't you see that?

CALVIN
Your mother doesn't hate you,
Conrad?

CONRAD
All right, all right. You're right.
She doesn't. Please leave me alone, now.
Silence. Then Calvin stands up and goes to the door.

CALVIN
What about this Dr. Berger? Do you think he's helping you?

CONRAD
Don't blame it on Burger, it's not his fault!
Calvin opens the door.

CALVIN
I'll be downstairs if you need me.
Exit Calvin. Conrad remains lying on his back with his arm over his eyes.
INT. Dr. BERGER'S OFFICE
- EVENING

DR BERGER
Tuesday you felt great. You bought a Christmas tree, it was all hunky- dory. Okay?

CONRAD
You're the doctor.

DR BERGER
Don't take refuge in one-liners like "You're the doctor". Okay?
Because that pisses me off.

CONRAD
Okay. Okay.

DR BERGER
So everything was fine till you had the fight with your mother, then everything was lousy.

CONRAD
Yeah, but I don't blame her. I mean, she's got... She's got her reasons. It's impossible after all the shit I've pulled!

DR BERGER
What shit have you pulled? Hey!
Remember! I'm talking proportion here. Now, what shit?
Conrad sighs.
DR BERGER (cont'd)
Come on. You must be able to come up with at least one example.
And don't give me "I tried to kill myself", that's old turkey.
What have you done lately?

CONRAD
Lately?

DR BERGER
Uh, uh.

CONRAD
Hey, come on, if you... Listen,
I'm never gonna be forgiven for that. Never! You know, you can't get it out, you know, all the blood in her towels, in her rug.
Everything had to be pitched.
Even the tiles in the bathroom had to be regrouted. Christ, she fired the godamn maid because she couldn't dust the living room right. If you think I'm gonna forgive... - that she's gonna forgive me...
Conrad stops. Dr. Berger looks at Conrad to signal him he just said something: Conrad realizes he just made a Freudian slip, looks at him,

DR BERGER
What?
Conrad stands up, reflects, looks outside window.

CONRAD
I think I just figured something out.

DR BERGER
What?

CONRAD
Who it is who can't forgive who...

DR BERGER
Well a real problem... a real problem has a real solution.

CONRAD
I've heard this all before.

DR BERGER
Doesn't make it any less true.

CONRAD
I'm so tired.

DR BERGER
Yeah, well... that's a hell of a secret you've been keeping on yourself.

CONRAD
So what do I do now?

DR BERGER
Recognize her limitations.

CONRAD
You mean, like she can't love me?

DR BERGER
Oh, kiddo, no. Like she can't love you enough. Like don't blame her for not loving you more than she's able.

CONRAD
But she loves my father. I know she loved my brother. It's me!

DR BERGER
Ha! Now we're back to the rotten kid routine! She can't love you because you're unlovable. Where does that leave your dad? How come he loves you? You're a rottenkid, doesn't he know that?

CONRAD
That's different. He feels responsible. Besides, he loves everybody.

DR BERGER
Ho, I get it! The guy's got no taste! He loves you, but he's wrong.
Look... maybe she just can't express it the way you'd like her to. Maybe she's just afraid to show you what she feels.

CONRAD
What do you mean?

DR BERGER
I mean there's someone besides your mother you've got to forgive.

CONRAD
You mean me?

Conrad is wondering.
CONRAD (cont'd)
For trying to off myself?
Don't you sit there and stare at me. What for?

DR BERGER
Why don't you give yourself a break? Let yourself off the hook?

CONRAD
What did I do?
No answer.
CONRAD (cont'd)
What did I do?

DR BERGER
We'll talk about it on Thursday.

CONRAD
Come on!

DR BERGER
Time's up.

CONRAD
What do you mean? You're gonna pull the plug... Come on! What did I do?

DR BERGER
Come on, Con. You know the rules.

CONRAD
Rules? What rules? Can't I have a few minutes?

DR BERGER
You think about it. Just think about it.
Silence

CONRAD
Jesus!
Conrad is out of breath.

EXT. PARK - DAY
Calvin and Friend are jogging in sportswear. Calvin's friend explains a stock market deal he made.

FRIEND

Say. After going to a new high, it falls to 112 1/4 and then rallies on good volume. I shoot an order to buy 4000 at the market. If I get the 4000 shares at 113 3/4, I know something's wrong.

(MORE)
FRIEND (cont'd)
But suppose the order to buy the
4000 shares I put in at the price of 113 3/4, I get 2000 at 114, 500 at 114 1/4, and the rest on the way up, so the last 500 shares I pay
115 1/2, then I know I'm right.I'm going to peel off here.
Friend leaves Calvin and runs toward his home.

CALVIN
OK.
FRIEND
I'll see you, Cal.

CALVIN
See you later.
Now Calvin is running through the park alone. Different voices are echoing off screen.

FRIEND
(OS)
Suppose the order to buy 4000 at

/..
BETH
(OS)
He walks all over us and you go up there and apologize to him...

FRIEND
(OS)
500 at 114...

CONRAD
(OS)
It's all German pudding with you, dad, you don't see things.

BETH
(OS)
You've been apologizing to him ever since he came home from the hospital. And you just don't see that!

CONRAD
(OS)
Tell her to stop it! You never tell her a godamn thing!

BETH
(OS)
Buck never would have been in the hospital!

CONRAD
(OS)
She hates me! Can't you see that?
Calvin trips, and falls in dead leaves. He sits up, thoughtfull.

CALVIN
(OS)
I want to be clear.
INT. Dr. BERGER'S OFFICE
- EVENING
Calvin laughs nervously, all smiles.

DR BERGER
(OS)
That's good.

CALVIN
In the car, I was thinking: "be clear.". I suppose that's what psychiatry's about. Being precise and clear. And honest, of course.
I'll level with you. I'm not a great believer in psychiatry.

DR BERGER
Okay.

CALVIN
I know what happens here is only between you and him, and...I like that, I respect that. And...he's better, I can see that. I am not trying to put you down, I just don't believe in psychiatry as a panacea for everybody.

DR BERGER
Neither do I.
Calvin laughs.

CALVIN
I wish I knew what the hell I was doing here.

DR BERGER
Well, you said you... thought you could shed some light on some things. What did you mean by that?

CALVIN

I don't know actually, I'm not sure, I think I meant in terms of Conrad. You see, I knew something was wrong even before he tried to... to kill himself. But I thought that... It's clear that he's very smart. He's been an "A" student ever since he started school, and naturally I thought that ...intelligent people could work out their own problems.

DR BERGER
But you still feel responsible?

CALVIN
Yeah, sure I do. It's hard not to.
It was luck. It was just luck that I happened to be there when he tried it. I could have been at a meeting. We both could've been away. It was luck!

DR BERGER
You think of yourself as a lucky man, then?

CALVIN
No! No. No. I used to. I used to think... that I was a lucky person... before... the "accident".
Mmm, I guess the whole of life is nothing but an accident, is it?
What happens to you. I should do with it.

DR BERGER
That sounds more like the philosophy of a drifter than a tax attorney.

CALVIN
Yeah. Maybe, maybe I am drifting a little. I can see myself, ...and I can see the two of them drifting away from me, and I just stand there watching.

DR BERGER
What would you want to do about that?

CALVIN
Something. I gotta do something about it. I don't know what.

(MORE)
CALVIN (cont'd)
I feel like I'm sitting on a fence, and I don't like it.

DR BERGER
And you see them as on ...opposite sides of this fence?

CALVIN
Yeah... No. I don't know. I see her not being able to forgive him.

DR BERGER
For what?

CALVIN
Oh, I don't know exactly. Being too much like her. People always think that she and Buck are... were
...were alike. But it's really she and Conrad. They were the only two that didn't cry at the funeral, you know? It's not easy for me to admit this but, uh... she didn't...
His mother doesn't show him a great deal of affection. I'm not trying to put her down in any way at all. She is a wonderful woman, huh...

DR BERGER
Did she give Buck much affection to
...Buck?

CALVIN
Oh, god, yes, she loved Buck!
Bucky got so much... I think what she felt for him was special. You know, he was her first-born.
That's not unusual, is it?

DR BERGER
And you?

CALVIN
Me? I loved Buck.

DR BERGER
What I mean is, your wife's affection.

CALVIN
For me you mean?

DR BERGER
Yes.

CALVIN
Mmm. She's very... No. There's no problem with her for me. We've been... We've been married nearly twenty one years. Everybody loves
Beth. But, huh... for Conrad, - it's been difficult. He didn't talk about that? We don't know what happens here. It doesn't come up. I guess that's what it is. It's private here. Isn't it?

DR BERGER
Mm-hmm. Very private.

CALVIN
I think I know why I came here. I think I came here to talk about myself.

DR BERGER
Okay. Why don't we?

INT. JARRETT'S HOME. GARAGE - NIGHT
Calvin sits in the dark in his car behind the wheel, not looking too happy. Door to garage opens and Beth appears.

BETH
Hi!
Calvin slowly opens the door. Car Buzzer Alarm. Calvin heavily comes out.
BETH (cont'd)
Calvin?
[Buzzing Continues]
BETH (cont'd)
What's the matter?
Calvin heavily comes out of the car, and finally closes door.
Buzzing stops.

CALVIN
This will sound strange.
What I'm gonna to say will sound strange.

BETH
What happened?
Come inside.

CALVIN
Could we talk about Buck's funeral?

BETH
What?

CALVIN
I know it'll seem trivial, but it's on my mind, or has been, and I'd just like to talk about it.

BETH
Why?

CALVIN
When I was getting dressed for
Buck's funeral, I was...

BETH
Calvin, what's the matter with you?

CALVIN
Just let me get it off my chest, OK?

BETH
What could getting dressed for
Buck's funeral possibly have to do with anything right now?

CALVIN
I was wearing a blue shirt. And you said: - Wear a white shirt and the other shoes!
It was nothing at the time. But it's always seemed to stay with me. And I, for some reason, been thinking about it and it suddenly occured to me what difference did it make what I wore at Buck's funeral?

BETH
Ha, ha.
Beth retreats inside the house to the kitchen.

CALVIN
Just hear me out, Beth! It won't hurt you to listen!

BETH
I won't listen to that! No one in their right mind would listen to that.

CALVIN
I just want to talk about something
I always remembered.

BETH
Why do you want to remind me of it?

CALVIN
Because I've always wondered, in some needling way, what it mattered what I wore. I was crazy that day.
We were going to our son's funeral.
And you were worried about what I wore on my feet. I'm sure it sounds like nothing to you, but it sticks with me and I just wanted to ...tell you about it.
She comes to him and takes him into her arms.

BETH
It's all right.

INT. MALL - DAY

Two stairways, one going down, one up, cross each other in the middle space of the mall. On the one going down is Beth,
Caroll, Beth's friend, is on the other. They have to shout.

CAROLL
Beth! Beth! Hi! How are you?

BETH
Caroll! I'm fine. How are you?

CAROLL
I haven't seen you!

BETH
I know. I'm so busy. I promise I'll call you soon and we'll have lunch.

CAROLL
Right!

BETH
How's Brad? Give him my love.

CAROLL
Fabulous! Is everything okay?
Beth gestures to the crowd in the mall.

BETH
Isn't this madness? It gets worse every year!
Good-bye!

CAROLL
Good-bye!

INT. MALL SHOP - DAY
Beth is spacing, seemingly gazing at a dress.

SALESWOMAN
May I show you this in your size?

BETH
What?

SALESWOMAN
May I show you this dress in your size?

BETH

Oh... No, no. No. Thanks.

INT. MALL DINER - DAY
Beth and Conrad are having lunch at a table in the diner.
Beth is summing up the birthday presents she bought.

BETH
We've got Bennett's, and Grant's and Foley's. Ha, Conrad should get something for my mother and father.
He's not supposed to get something for his doctor, is he?

CALVIN
I don't think so. I think we should go see him, Beth. - Dr. Berger.
Beth laughs.

BETH
What?

CALVIN
I think we could all go and see him together.

BETH
Why?

CALVIN
He thinks it's a good idea.

BETH
Ho... He thinks it's a good idea?
What does he know about me, about this family? I've never even met him.

CALVIN
Exactly. That's the point.
Wouldn't it be easier if we all talked about it? In the open.

BETH
About what? What are we gonna talk about? Don't try to change me,
Calvin. I don't want anymore changes in my life. For God's sake, hasn't enough happened? Let's just hold on to what we've got!

CALVIN
Darling, that is what this is for.
Maybe you'll get a surprise.

BETH
I don't want any surprises.

I know I'm not perfect. And if I can't go around hugging everybody all the time the way you do, then
I'm sorry.

CALVIN
I am not asking you to be perfect, you're missing the point.

BETH
I don't want to see any doctors or counselors. I am me. This is my family. And if we have problems, then we will solve those problems in the privacy of our own home, not by running to some kind of specialist everytime something goes wrong...

WAITRESS
(interrupting)
Are you folks ready to order?

CALVIN
Huh, no... Could you give me a couple of minutes, please?

WAITRESS
Sure.

BETH
...running to experts every time something goes wrong.
Silence
BETH (cont'd)
I know you mean well. I want this to be a nice Christmas.

CALVIN
I do too. I want all of them to be nice Christmases

BETH
We need time together, Calvin. You and I. We have to get away. New
Years'. We can spend some time in
Houston with my brother and Audrey.
You know, play a little golf.
Relax.
Calvin seems doubtfull. Beth goes softly.
BETH (cont'd)
I have already talked to Mother about it, and Conrad can stay with them. Please don't worry about it.
Please, for his sake, don't indulge him. We need time together. Okay?

CALVIN
Okay. Okay.
Beth takes his hand but it seems almost like a handshake.

BETH
I love you.

CALVIN
I love you, too.
Beth stares at him.

BETH
Let's just give things time. Okay?
Calvin doesn't say anything.

EXT. JEANNINE'S HOME - EVENING NIGHT
Conrad came to pick her up, they both come out. Conrad fetches his car keys while she closes her door.

JEANNINE
Conrad?

CONRAD
Hmm?

JEANNINE
I don't bowl. I mean, I'm a horrible bowler.

CONRAD
Oh, that's all right.

JEANNINE
Yeah. Well...
Conrad wants to open the door on her side.
JEANNINE (cont'd)
I got it. That's OK. Thing is,
I'm a funny bowler.

CONRAD
Well, listen. We don't have to go bowling if you'd rather not, I'm not a bowling nut or anything. How funny are you?

JEANNINE
On a scale from one to ten? ...
About a ten.

CONRAD
Hoo, that's pretty funny. Hey, well, listen, I promise you won't look silly.

JEANNINE
Guarantee it?

CONRAD
Guarantee it.
They get into the car.

INT. BOWLING ALLEY - NIGHT.
Jeannine enters frame looking very focused, ball in hand.
Conrad looks. She shoots but the ball drops and goes into the gutter to the end. Conrad does not react. The skittles are intact.

INT. DINER - NIGHT.
Jeannine is eating a hamburger.

JEANNINE
Can you ever break the ball?

CONRAD
Can't break the ball, can't break the floor, can't break anything in a bowling alley. And that's what I like about bowling alleys. Can't even break the record.
Jeannine giggles with laughing eyes.
CONRAD (cont'd)
Anyway...

JEANNINE
Hmm? What?

CONRAD
Just "anyway", it's a conversation starter.

JEANNINE
Catchy!

CONRAD
You like it?

JEANNINE
Mmm, mmm.

CONRAD
I thought it'd get to you. I've been working on it all day.
Jeannine laughs, then:

JEANNINE
Do you think people are punished for the things they do?

CONRAD
You mean by God?

JEANNINE
Yeah.

CONRAD
Mmm, I don't believe in God.

JEANNINE
Not at all?

CONRAD
No. Well, it's not a question of degree. Either you do or you don't.

JEANNINE
I believe in God.

CONRAD
So you're afraid he'll punish you for something you did?

JEANNINE
I've done a lot of things I'm ashamed of.

CONRAD
Yeah? So have I.
She looks up at him, then at his wrists.

JEANNINE
Did it hurt?

CONRAD
No, I dunno, I don't remember really.

JEANNINE
You don't want to talk about it?

CONRAD
Ah, I don't know... I've never really talked about it.
To doctors, but not to anyone else.
You're the first who's asked.

JEANNINE
Why did you do it?

CONRAD
Uh... I don't know. It was like... falling into a hole.
It was like falling into a hole, and it keeps getting bigger and bigger, .and you can't get out, and then, .all of a sudden, it's inside...and you're the hole, and you're trapped, and it's all over. Something like that. And it's not really scary, except it is when you think back on it.
'Cause you know what you were feeling stange and new...
A group of noisy students enter the Diner.

STUDENTS
(singing and horsing around)

(MORE)
STUDENTS (cont'd)
Like McDonald's can, nobody can do it. Like McDonald's can, you deserve a break today. So get up and get away!
The manager tries to calm them down. A student comes to
Conrad's table and steals some fries.

STUDENT
Hey. Jarrett. How you doing? How about some fries?
Some students grab Jeannine and dance around, put a Mac donald's hat on her head. She laughs.

JEANNINE
What are you doing?
The manager pushes them towards the exit.

STUDENT
Hey, what's your problem? Lighten up!

MANAGER
Hey. I don't like your attitude.
Going out, a student pulls the manager's ear. Jeannine laughs, a bit stupidly. Conrad notices it. She sees that.

INT. CAR - NIGHT
Conrad drives sadly. He is disappointed and acts as if he was sulking. Jeannine tries to make it up.

JEANNINE
Energetic. Those guys.

CONRAD
(not believing)
Yeah, they were pretty funny.

JEANNINE
No...

CONRAD
What? You thought they were funny?

JEANNINE
No. I...
Silence
JEANNINE (cont'd)
I'm sorry, I...

CONRAD
What for?

JEANNINE
Anyway...
Conrad does not find this funny. Finally car stops. Conrad sighs.
JEANNINE (cont'd)
Do you want to talk?

CONRAD
About what?

JEANNINE
Are you okay?

CONRAD
Yeah. Yeah, I'm fine. Uh... I'll give you a call.

JEANNINE
Will you? I want you to.

CONRAD
Sure.

JEANNINE
Well... Guess I'll see you in choir.

CONRAD
Okay. Yeah. Thanks.

JEANNINE
Okay.

CONRAD
I mean. Good night. Good night.

JEANNINE
Good night.
Jeannine leaves the car.

INT. JET - DAY
Beth is all smiles, she succeeded with Calvin. They both are playing with their earphone

CALVIN
Seven.

BETH
Yes... It's not even plugged in.
Stewardess' voice in loudspeaker.

STEWARDESS
In preparation for our landing in
Houston, observe the fasten seat belt sign......

EXT. JET �DAY
Jet lands on Huston's airport runway.

STEWARDESS
......and please no smoking until well inside the terminal. Thank you.

EXT. HUSTON GOLF - AFTERNOON
Golf ball being wished out of sight by a club. Beth, Calvin,
Ward (Beth's brother) and his wife Audrey, are having drinks sitting at a table on a golf course under a parasol.
WARD lifts his golf club and demonstrates a clumsy hesitating swing, and how it misses.

WARD
Watch this. Pessimistic golfer.
Pessimistic golfer.
Ward arms his club as if to strike, then stops.
WARD (cont'd)
Oh. Damn!
They laugh.
WARD (cont'd)
Are we two up? Two?

GOLF PLAYER
(OS)

Two!

WARD
All right. Let's hustle up. We're close here.

CALVIN
I'll never get over how flat it is here. I'll never get over...

WARD
I know it's flat, but we decided to teach you to love it.

AUDREY
He is trying to get everybody to move down here.

BETH
Really?

AUDREY
Gosh, you guys, it's so good to see you. You look tired. Cal.

CALVIN
Airplane scotch.

BETH
Would you tell me why it is I am still hungry?

WARD
'Cause you're in Texas, girl.
When we get done, we'll get you home. Get ya some steaks on the barbecue. Audrey will put together her famous salad.

BETH
With baked potatoe and sour cream, too, uh? How long has he had that drawl?

AUDREY
Ever since we joined the country club.

INT. SWIMMING POOL - NIGHT
Revolver fires upwards. Swimmers dive. It's a swimming competition. Conrad is sitting on one of the top bleachers, fully dressed, uneasy, while down there, by the side of the pool, his friends, in swimming trunks and wet hair, watch the race. Lazenby sees him, Conrad looks down. In the audience, everyone is shouting for his team.

.../...

Now the competition is finished. The swimming pool is empty and silent, except for someone sweeping the side of the pool, and Conrad sitting still, reflecting, looking around.

EXT. SWIMMING POOL EXIT - NIGHT
The group comes out of the pool. Conrad at the back, as if he wasn't part of it.

LAZENBY
I am glad you can laugh about it, cos' it sure as hell wasn't funny.
Come on, we weren't that bad.

STILLMAN
Let's face it, we stunk.
I don't know how you can listen to that lecture on Buck Jarrett one more time.
I know he is the world's greatest swimmer, but it bugs the hell outa me when he does that.

LAZENBY
Stillman, cut it.

STILLMAN
Think he's ever gonna stop kissing the guy's picture?

LAZENBY
Stillman, shut the hell up, would you? Hey, con, you want a ride?

CONRAD
Oh. No. Thanks.

LAZENBY
We sure could've used you today, buddy.

CONRAD
Oh, no, I don't think so.

LAZENBY
Yeah... I don't think anybody could've helped us today.

STILLMAN
How's it going, Jarrett? I hear you got eyes for Pratt these days. You in her pants yet?

CONRAD
Hey, do me a favor, Stillman, try not to be such a prick.

STILLMAN
You're the prick. Guys like you walk around like you're king shit.

94

You give me a goddamn pain in the ass, you think we owe you...
Conrad hits him hard with a jab, then jumps on him. They fall in the plastic bags of the disposal, Conrad still hitting.
Lazenby tries to stop him. Conrad pushes him away. Two students take hold of Conrad and pull him away, two others with Stillman.

LAZENBY
Come on! Connie. Come on! Cool it,
Jarrett! Connie! Connie. That's enough.

STUDENTS
No, Stillman, no! No!

STILLMAN
Let go! Let go!

LAZENBY
It's all right! He's crazy! Just calm down, uh?

STILLMAN
You're crazy! You're crazy! You know that?
Conrad walks back to his car
STILLMAN (cont'd)
Send him back where he came from!

OTHERS
Now, now, it's over. It's over.

STILLMAN
All right! Shit!
Stillman hits a garbage bag.

INT. CAR - NIGHT
Conrad opens the door and sits down in his car. Lazenby comes, opens the door and hands Conrad his hat.

LAZENBY
Here's your hat.
Lazenby comes in and sits.
LAZENBY (cont'd)
You want to talk? The guy's a nothing. He's a zero upstairs.
You used to know that about him,
Con. Ever since fourth grade, you've known it.

CONRAD
So?

LAZENBY
So you just make yourself look stupid when you let him get to you like that!

CONRAD
So I look stupid, is that it?

LAZENBY
No, it isn't. What is it with you?
Huh? I don't know why you want to be in this alone? You know, I miss him too. Connie, the three of us were best friends!

CONRAD
I can't help it, it hurts too much to be around you. I gotta go.
Lazenby looks at him, then opens the door and goes out.

LAZENBY
Yeah. Okay.
Conrad remains alone and touches the horn by accident.

INT. GRANDPARENTS' HOME, STAIRS & LANDING - NIGHT
Conrad gets home, climbs upstairs directly to his room, and closes the door. His grandmother hears him, opens her bedroom door, closes it.

INT. CONRAD'S BEDROOM - NIGHT
Conrad reflects for a short time, then goes down to...

INT. KITCHEN - NIGHT
Conrad enters the kitchen, takes something in the fridge, goes to the phone to make a call. He dials.

KAREN'S MOTHER (OS)
Hello?

CONRAD
Hello. Is Karen there?

KAREN'S MOTHER (OS)
She...uh... Ah!... Bill?

KAREN'S FATHER (OS)
Hello.

CONRAD
Yes, hello. Is Karen there? This is
Conrad Jarrett, calling. I'm a friend of hers.

KAREN'S FATHER CONRAD
Karen's... I called...

KAREN'S FATHER
Karen's dead.

CONRAD
What? What?

KAREN'S FATHER
She killed herself.
Karen's father hangs up. Conrad suffocates under the shock.
He hears Karen's voice.

KAREN
(OS)
Let's have the best Christmas ever.

INT. BATHROOM - NIGHT
Conrad rushes into the bathroom

CONRAD
Ha!

INT. RESTAURANT - DAY
[Very short flashback on Karen]

KAREN
We can. You know.

INT. BATHROOM - NIGHT
Conrad has rushed into the bathroom where he ends up sitting on the toilet and grabbing the washbowl, out of breath under the shock.

KAREN
(OS)
We could have the best year of our whole lives.
Conrad opens tap, water flows.

EXT. LAKE - NIGHT
[Flashback to the boat accident on the lake] Conrad yells at
Buck (who is holding tight the rope maintaining the sail up) to have him get the sail down; but Buck is stubborn and asks Conrad (who is at the helm) to maintain starboard course.[The result of opposites will overturn the small boat]. Waves of water

CONRAD
Get the sail down! Get it down!

BUCK
I can't hold it! Keep it starboard!

INT. KITCHEN - NIGHT
Conrad stares at himself in the mirror

EXT. LAKE - NIGHT
CONRAD
Get the sail down! Get it down!

BUCK
Keep it starboard!

INT. BATHROOM - NIGHT
Conrad takes water in his hands...

EXT. LAKE - NIGHT
BUCK
Go for it!

CONRAD
I am trying! I can't! Let it out!

INT. BATHROOM - NIGHT
Conrad stares at the water in his hands

EXT. LAKE - NIGHT
CONRAD
Let it out!

BUCK
Just keep it starboard!

CONRAD
I can't!
Boat overturns.
CONRAD (cont'd)
Ahh!

BUCK
Ahh!

INT. STAIRS - NIGHT

Conrad rushes downstairs with his coat.

EXT. LAKE - NIGHT
Conrad comes out from underwater, taking air in.

CONRAD
Aaah!

INT. STAIRS - NIGHT
Conrad rushes downstairs with his coat.

EXT. LAKE - NIGHT
CONRAD
Bucky!

BUCK
Give me your hand!

CONRAD
Here!

EXT. HOUSE - NIGHT
Conrad rushes out of the house.

EXT. LAKE - NIGHT
The boys are holding each other's hands over the overturned boat's hull.

BUCK
We screwed up this time, Buddy!
Dad's gonna haul ass over this!

CONRAD
It ain't so goddamned funny!

EXT. STREET - NIGHT
Conrad rushes.

EXT. LAKE - NIGHT
BUCK
Just don't let go!

CONRAD
I won't, honest to God!

BUCK
Everything gonna be okay!

EXT. STREET - NIGHT
Conrad rushes.

EXT. LAKE - NIGHT
BUCK
Hang on. Brother!
But Buck's wet hand slips away. Buck tries to gain hold on the curved slippery surface of the hull, but he can't make it and disappears into the water, while Conrad manages somehow to hold on.

CONRAD
Stay with me! Stay with me!
Stay with me! Bucky! Where are you?
Buck disappears into water.

EXT. STREET - NIGHT
Conrad rushes.

EXT. LAKE - NIGHT
CONRAD
Bucky!

EXT. STREET - NIGHT
Conrad rushes.

EXT. LAKE - NIGHT
Conrad holds on firmly to keel of boat

CONRAD
Bucky!

EXT. STREET - NIGHT
Conrad rushes.

EXT. LAKE - NIGHT
Conrad holds on firmly to keel of boat

CONRAD
Buck!

EXT. STREET - NIGHT
Conrad rushes.

EXT. LAKE - NIGHT
Conrad holds on firmly to keel of boat

CONRAD
Buck!

STREET - NIGHT
Conrad runs, gets to a phone booth, calls Dr Berger, out of breath.

DR BERGER
(OS, drowsy)
Hello?

CONRAD
This is Conrad!

DR BERGER
What's going on?

CONRAD
I need to see you!

DR BERGER
What time is it?

CONRAD
I don't know!

DR BERGER
Where are you?

CONRAD
I... I don't know!

DR BERGER
All right. Listen to me. Get to the office somehow, and I'll meet you there.

CONRAD
Okay.

INT. DR BERGER'S OFFICE LIFT & CORRIDOR - NIGHT
Dr Berger comes out of the lift and finds Conrad waiting in the dark corridor, in a state of emotional shock.

DR BERGER
Oh, good. You're here.

CONRAD

Something happened...
Dr Berger fiddles for his keys in the dark to open his office's door.

DR BERGER
Just wait, just hold on...

CONRAD
I need... I need...

DR BERGER
Just wait till we get inside...
Dr Berger finally opens the door. They enter.
DR BERGER (cont'd)
There...

INT. DR BERGER'S OFFICE
Dr Berger enters the dark office

DR BERGER
Shit. You'd think they'd assume there'd be an emergency now and then?!
DR BERGER (cont'd)
Don't take it off. Just sit down.
Conrad cries.

CONRAD
Something happened!

DR BERGER
What?

CONRAD
It's...

DR BERGER
It's what?

CONRAD
Oh. God! I need something.

DR BERGER
What do you need? Tell me!

CONRAD
It just keeps coming! I can't... I can't make it stop!

DR BERGER

Don't try.

CONRAD
I gotta... I gotta... I gotta get off the hook for it. I gotta get off the hook!

DR BERGER
For what?

CONRAD
For what I did!

DR BERGER
What did you do?

CONRAD
What I did to him!

DR BERGER
What did you do?

CONRAD
It's something... It's something...
Don't you see? It's gotta be somebody's fault or there's no godamm point!

DR BERGER
Point? What point? It happened!

CONRAD
No, no... Oh, no. I don't mean that. It's that... It's just that... Buck, Bucky, I didn't mean it!

EXT. LAKE - NIGHT
Flash of Buck in storm.

INT. DR BERGER'S OFFICE
CONRAD
Bucky, I didn't mean it!

EXT. LAKE - NIGHT
Flash of Buck in storm.

INT. DR BERGER'S OFFICE
CONRAD
Bucky!

DR BERGER

I know that, it wasn't your fault.

CONRAD
But it was: you said. "Get the sail down!" ...

EXT. LAKE - NIGHT
Flash on both hands of Conrad holding tight the rudder

CONRAD
...and I couldn't!

INT. DR BERGER'S OFFICE
CONRAD
I couldn't! It jammed! And then the halyard, the halyard jammed! I couldn't because the godamn halyard jammed! And then you're sittin' here, you're screwing around...

EXT. LAKE - NIGHT
Flash of Buck in water trying to hold on overturned boat.

INT. DR BERGER'S OFFICE
CONRAD
...until it's too late to do anything! And I'm supposed to take care of it!

EXT. LAKE - NIGHT
Flash of Conrad giving Buck a hand over the overturned hull of the boat.

CONRAD
And I'm supposed to take care of it!

INT. DR BERGER'S OFFICE
DR BERGER
And that wasn't fair, was it?

CONRAD
No! And then you say ...

EXT. LAKE - NIGHT
Flash of Conrad holding Buck's hand.

CONRAD
(OS)
"Hang on!"...

INT. DR BERGER'S OFFICE
CONRAD
..."Hang on!", and then you let go!

EXT. LAKE - NIGHT
Flash : hands separating

INT. DR BERGER'S OFFICE
CONRAD
Why'd you let go?

DR BERGER
Because I got tired!

CONRAD
Yeah? Well. Screw you, you jerk!
Conrad breaks down and cries.

DR BERGER
It hurts to be mad at him, doesn't it?

CONRAD
Yeah. He just wasn't careful. He just wouldn't care. He didn't see how a bad thing might happen.

DR BERGER
Bad things happen even when people are careful.

CONRAD
We were screwing around out there, we should've come in when it started to look bad.

DR BERGER
OK, so you made a mistake.

CONRAD
Why did he let go? Why?

DR BERGER
Maybe you were stronger. Did it ever occur to you that you might have been stronger?
Conrad comes out of it and stares at him.
DR BERGER (cont'd)
How long you gonna punish yourself?
When you gonna quit?

CONRAD
Oh, God, I'd like to quit.

DR BERGER
Why don't you?

CONRAD
It's not easy. It's not that easy.
God... I loved him.

DR BERGER
I know.
Dr Berger takes off his coat, sits down. Calvin cries.
DR BERGER (cont'd)
What happened? You said something happened. What started all this?
Calvin stutters with pain and cries.

CONRAD
Ka-ren. She killed herself! I just found out she's dead.

DR BERGER
Jesus.

CONRAD
And she was fine, she was OK.

DR BERGER
No. She wasn't.

CONRAD
She was! She was! She told me! She said she was...

DR BERGER
What?

CONRAD
She was busy, she was feeling good and she...

DR BERGER
And what?
Conrad cries.
DR BERGER (cont'd)
What?

CONRAD
I just wish I'd known...I could've done something.

DR BERGER
You saw her once and now you' want to take her on too?

CONRAD

No!

DR BERGER
No?

CONRAD
No. I just...

DR BERGER
What?

CONRAD
That isn't it. I... I feel bad about this, I feel really bad about this. And just let me feel bad about this!

DR BERGER
Okay. Listen. I feel bad about it too.

CONRAD
Why do things have to happen to people? It isn't fair.

DR BERGER
You're right. It isn't fair.

CONRAD
You just do one wrong thing... and...

DR BERGER
Um-hmm.
And what was the one wrong thing you did?

EXT. LAKE - NIGHT
Flash of Conrad looking around in the water for Buck.

CONRAD
(OS)
Haaa...

INT. DR BERGER'S OFFICE
DR BERGER
You know.
Conrad looks at him and cries and sighs.

EXT. LAKE - NIGHT
Flash of Conrad getting back on hull and clutching to the keel.

CONRAD
(OS)
Haaa...

INT. DR BERGER'S OFFICE
Conrad stares at Dr Berger.

CONRAD
Haaa...

DR BERGER
You know.

EXT. LAKE - NIGHT
Flash of Conrad clutching to the keel.

CONRAD
(OS)
Haaa...

INT. DR BERGER'S OFFICE
Conrad stares at Dr Berger.

CONRAD
I hung on. I stayed with the boat.

DR BERGER
Exactly.
Conrad cries.

EXT. LAKE - NIGHT
Flash of Conrad clutching to the keel.

CONRAD
(OS)
Haaa...

INT. DR BERGER'S OFFICE
DR BERGER
Now. You can live with that. Can't you?

EXT. LAKE - NIGHT
Flash of Conrad clutching to the keel. Waves.

CONRAD
(OS)

Haaa...

INT. DR BERGER'S OFFICE
Conrad cries

CONRAD
I'm scared! I'm scared.

DR BERGER
Feelings are scary. And sometimes they're painful. And if you can't feel pain, then you're not gonna feel anything else either. You know what I'm saying?

CONRAD
I think so.

DR BERGER
You're here and you're alive. And don't tell me you don't feel that.

CONRAD
It doesn't feel good.

DR BERGER
It is good. Believe me.

CONRAD
How do you know?

DR BERGER
Because I'm your friend.
Conrad is out of breath.

CONRAD
I don't know what I would've done...if you hadn't been here.
You're really my friend?

DR BERGER
I am. Count on it.
Conrad falls into Dr Berger's arms, crying.

EXT. JEANNINE'S HOME - EARLY MORNING
Jeannine opens her curtains, sees Conrad, outside her home, walking to and fro. She puts on a jacket and comes out to him.

CONRAD
Hi. I was gonna call but I didn't want to wake anyone.

JEANNINE
Might have been easier...

CONRAD
Listen, I want to say something about the other night. I mean I liked being with you but I didn't like myself.

JEANNINE
Conrad. I was stupid.
That was dumb of me to laugh and it was my fault. I just didn't know what to do. I was embarrassed.

CONRAD
Really? You were embarrassed?

JEANNINE
Yes. When those boys came in, it was awful and awkward. That's what I do when I get embarrassed. I laugh.

CONRAD
But they were all right. They were just up and they were having a good time, and I let them get in the way of what was happening. It was dumb.
It was dumb. I've been doing lots of dumb things lately. I just didn't know wether or not you were being straight with me.
Jeannine is moved, she extends her hand to him then put it to her heart.
CONRAD (cont'd)
Yeah?
Jeannine nods.
CONRAD (cont'd)
Anyway, I'd like to try it again. I thought it worked out okay. Well, except for the bowling.
Jeannine laughs, looks down, then looks up straight in his eyes.

JEANNINE
Yes.

CONRAD
Yes?
Jeannine nods.

JEANNINE
Yes.
Conrad is moved.

CONRAD
Uh... Are you going to school?

JEANNINE
No, not on Sunday.
Conrad realizes. Laughs.
JEANNINE (cont'd)
Have you eaten?

CONRAD
No. I haven't.

JEANNINE
Do you want some breakfast?
Conrad nods. She smiles at him.

CONRAD
Okay.
They go up the steps and Jeannine opens the screen door.

JEANNINE
Mom!

EXT. HUSTON GOLF - AFTERNOON
(CU) Golf ball falls into hole.

WARD
Oh !...

BETH
All right. How about that?

CALVIN
Boy, oh, boy.
Beth is beaming from her success at golf.

BETH
Oh, I do love that.

CALVIN
Oh, these holes sure do love you.
Oh boy, oh boy.

BETH
We should spend more time playing golf together, you know that?
Maybe our next vacation, strictly golf. Pinehurst, Myrtle Beach...

CALVIN

Pinehurst would be nice. I think
Connie would like Pinehurst.
She pulls back and looks at him.

BETH
Do you do that deliberately or is it just a reflex?

CALVIN
Well, you said "vacation", so I just assumed you meant him too.

BETH
I'm surprised you haven't felt the need to call him since we've been here.

CALVIN
I was gonna call him tonight.

BETH
(to Ward and Audrey)
Hey, could we have a little drink before we head back?

WARD
Drink, yes. Little, no.
(to Calvin)
What'd you get? Cal, what'd you get?

CALVIN
(to Ward)
Six.
(to Beth)
Let's finish this.

BETH
What?

CALVIN
What you started.

BETH
What I started?

CALVIN
What you started.

BETH
Ha! There's no point discussing it.

CALVIN
I think there is a point.

BETH
He controls you even when you are two thousand miles away.

CALVIN
He isn't the problem.

BETH
Isn't he?

CALVIN
No, he isn't. Let's talk about what's really bothering you.

BETH
No, no. Let's talk about what's bothering you. Cos' that's what you want, isn't it?

CALVIN
Jesus, what have I done to make you so angry with me?

BETH
It's not what you've done, it's what you think I've done. You blame me for the whole thing.

CALVIN
Can't you see anything except in terms of how it affects you?

BETH
No! I can't! And neither can you, and neither can anybody else! Only maybe I'm just a little more honest about it!

CALVIN
Well, stop being so godamn honest, and start being a little generous! And start thinking about him for a while!

BETH
I don't know what he expects from me. I never have known.

CALVIN
Well, I'll tell you what he expects!

BETH
What? He wants me to throw my arms around him everytime he passes an exam? Well, I can't do it! I cannot respond when someone says:
"Here, I just did this great thing.

Love me.". I can't!

CALVIN
All he wants... All he wants is to know you don't hate him. That's it.

BETH
Hate him? My God! How could I hate him? Mothers don't hate their sons! Is that what he told you? Do you see how you accept what he says with no questions, and you can't do the same thing to me, can you?

CALVIN
I just try to keep this family together...

BETH
(she shouts)
I don't know what everyone wants from me anymore!

AUDREY
Beth, nobody wants anything from you.

WARD
Beth, listen. We all just want...
Cal, Con, everybody, we just want you to be happy.

BETH
Happy?

WARD
Yes.

BETH
Ward, you tell me the definition of happy, uh? But first, you better make sure that your kids are good and safe, that no one's fallen off a horse, or been hit by a car, or drowned in that swimming pool you're so proud of! And then you come to me and tell me how to be happy!
She leaves. Calvin follows. Ward and his wife just stand there.

INT. JET ◆ DAY
Beth stares away from Calvin, as in a void. She sighs, closes her eyes; Calvin turns away from the window, looks at Beth and remembers...
When they were happily dancing... [to and fro twice]
Calvin in his plane seat, reflects.

INT. LIVING ROOM - NIGHT
Beth checks a pile of mail. Conrad comes in.

CONRAD
I think I'm gonna turn in.
Dinner was good.
Really good.

CALVIN
It's pretty early. You tired?

CONRAD
Yeah. It was kind of a rough week.

CALVIN
I hope your grandmother wasn't too tough on you?

CONRAD
No. She was fine. I'm glad you're back.
Conrad gives his mother a hug, but she is like made of stone.
Calvin sees it.
CONRAD (cont'd)
Good night.
Beth remains transfixed as if she didn't know what it was all about. Calvin sees it.

INT. BEDROOM - NIGHT
Beth is not sleeping, she looks up, sees her husband wrinkled pillow, but he is not in bed. She looks at the time, gets up, puts on a robe.

INT. STAIRS - NIGHT
Beth goes downstairs, tying up her robe. She stops, hearing someone sobbing in the dark, in the dining room.

INT. DINING ROOM - NIGHT
Beth enters the dining room in the dark.

BETH
Calvin?
Calvin is sitting at table in the dark, sobbing, his head in his hands.
BETH (cont'd)
Why are you crying?
Calvin doesn't answer.
BETH (cont'd)
Can I, uh... Can I get you something?
Calvin mutters in a very low voice.

CALVIN
I don't...

BETH
What did you say?
Calvin sits back in his chair.
BETH (cont'd)
Calvin. What did you say?
Calvin produces a very deep sigh.
BETH (cont'd)
Tell me.
Calvin looks up at her with a sad expression.

CALVIN
You are beautiful. And you are unpredictable. But you're so cautious. You're determined, Beth.
But you know something? You're not strong. And I don't know if you're really giving.
Beth is looking at him not knowing what this is about.
CALVIN (cont'd)
Tell me something. Do you love me?
Do you really love me?

BETH
I feel the way I've always felt about you.
Calvin is disappointed by the answer, but not surprised, just sad.

CALVIN
We would've been all right, if there hadn't been any ...mess.
But you can't handle mess.
You need everything neat and
...easy.
I don't know. Maybe you can't love anybody. It was so much
Buck. And Buck died, it was as if you buried all your love with him, and I don't understand that.
I just don't know.
Calvin sighs.
CALVIN (cont'd)
Maybe it wasn't even Buck.
Maybe it was just you.
Maybe, finally, it was the best of you that you buried.

(MORE)
CALVIN (cont'd)
But whatever it was, I don't know who you are.
I don't know what we've been playing at.
So I was crying.
Calvin is overcome by sadness
CALVIN (cont'd)
't know if I love you anymore. And

I don't know what I am going to do without that.
Beth does not know what to say or do. She turns away and goes upstairs.

INT. BEDROOM - NIGHT
Beth enters, kind of reflects, then goes open a closet, takes out some luggage. A sudden burst of emotion overcomes her, she cries but does not seem to identify the emotion, then restrains it.

INT. CONRAD'S BEDROOM - DAWN
In his bed Conrad is not sleeping. He hears the door of the house close, then someone walking outside on the gravel. He gets up, go look out of the window. Ouside, a taxi leaves. He goes downstairs.

INT. STAIRS - DAWN
Conrad goes downstairs, curious. Looks around, sees nobody.

EXT. GARDEN - DAWN
From inside, Conrad finally sees his father in the garden, reflecting. Patches of snow. Conrad puts on his coat over his pyjamas, and joins him.

CONRAD
Dad?

CALVIN
The yard looks smaller without leaves.

CONRAD
Dad? What happened?

CALVIN
Your mother's going away for a while.

CONRAD
Where? Why?

CALVIN
Back to Houston.
Then I... I don't know.

CONRAD
Why? What... I know why. It's me.
Isn't it?

CALVIN
No.

CONRAD
Yeah, it is. It's my fault.

CALVIN
Don't do that! Don't do that to yourself! It's nobody's fault!
Things happen in this world, people don't always have answers for them, you know.
Calvin sits down.
CALVIN (cont'd)
I don't know why I'm yelling at you for...

CONRAD
No, that's right! You're right! You ought to do that more often.

CALVIN
Oh, yeah?

CONRAD
Yeah, yeah, Haul my ass a little, you know. Get after me. The way you used to for him.

CALVIN
Oh, he needed it. You didn't. You were always so hard on yourself, I never had the heart.

CONRAD
Oh, Dad. Don't.

CALVIN
No, it's the truth. I... I never worried about you. I just wasn't listening.

CONRAD
Well, I wasn't putting out many signals then. I don't think you could have done anything.

CALVIN
No, no, no, I should ...I should've got a handle on it somehow.

CONRAD
You know, I used to figure you had a handle for everything. You knew it all.
Calvin looks at him and laughs briefly at himself.
CONRAD (cont'd)
I know that wasn't fair but you always made us feel like everything was gonna be all right. I thought about that a lot lately. I really admire you for it.
Calvin is moved.

CALVIN
Well, don't admire people too much.
They'll disappoint you sometimes.

CONRAD
I'm not disappointed.
I love you.
Calvin looks at him, cries and takes him in his arms.

CALVIN
I love you too.
They hug each other.
[Camera pulls back / Canon in D by Pachelbel]
Credits roll.

THE END

Printed in Great Britain
by Amazon